Planting and Growing a Fundamental Church

by
Roy L. Thomas

Randall House Publications
114 Bush Road—P.O. Box 17306
Nashville, Tennessee 37217
1979

PLANTING AND GROWING A FUNDAMENTAL CHURCH
© Copyright 1979
Randall House Publications
Nashville, Tennessee

Printed in the United States of America

ISBN No. 0-89265-070-2

TABLE OF CONTENTS

To Pat

To the divinely chosen companion
of my life, the reality of my fondest
dreams, the reflector of her Savior's
image, my beautiful wife, I dedicate
this book in appreciation for the
countless hours spent in gathering
material for me, typing the manuscript,
and proofing the text.

INTRODUCTION

The author of this book is truly a *man of experience* in the field of home missions and church extension. He is a product of God's grace through a home missionary. Practically all of his adult life has been devoted to some phase of the ministry of home missions.

The Apostle Paul in his writings stressed both creed and conduct, doctrine and deportment, the theoretical as well as the practical. The author of this present work has followed Paul's noble example by stating clearly the theoretical and then carefully detailing the practical outworking of the principles of church planting.

Brother Thomas has *lived* this book. The procedures outlined were discovered as he served as a church planter. This is no "childless parent" telling parents with children how to raise a family. But rather, here is one who speaks with the voice of authority saying that this will work because he has already tested it in his own experience.

The writer of this book is a present day missionary. He has not only pioneered and blazed a trail, he has also written down a precise blueprint which will guide others. This book is surely sent out with the hope that many will follow who will plant local churches which will be productive until the Lord returns.

This book should certainly be required reading for every home missionary or church planter. It would be helpful for every foreign missionary to read it also, as the basic principles of church planting do not change. And too, many of the approaches suggested could be used on any mission field. The young pastor starting out should, by all means, read this work. The man who has already pastored should find this book refreshing as well as stimulating. The pastor will find concepts, ideas, and methods, some of which might bring new life to his ministry. Even the local church member who reads this book could learn how to serve the Lord better in his own church.

It is my hope that this book will be widely read and that God will be honored, when as a result of these pages, new churches are planted and present churches are strengthened.

—Charles A. Thigpen

Preface

The subject of this writing is planting and growing a fundamental church. The word "planting" refers to the beginning of the church by the church planter. How this should be done is described.

The word "growing" refers to the tedious process of building the church from the beginning stage to maturity. This makes the information contained valuable not only to church extension workers, but pastors as well who want their churches to grow.

The word "fundamental" denotes the beloved denomination which brought the author to Christ, built him up in the faith, and allowed him to serve for a quarter of a century. Free Will Baptists, the largest group of Arminian Baptists in the world, have been a spiritual force in America since 1727. It is hoped that this volume will inspire some to begin like churches in the cities of America and inspire others to strengthen the 2,500 existing such churches.

Reasons for the Study

This study was begun with a definite purpose in mind. There are few books in print on the subject of church planting. There is no work in print written distinctively for our churches.

From the church planting standpoint, there is a two-fold reason for this writing. First, the importance of planting fundamental, Bible believing, Bible practicing churches across America needs to be published to challenge qualified men to engage in this work. Second, those men engaged in church planting, either as home missionaries, or as "tent makers," need a manual from which they can receive information on the proper methods to be used.

From the church growth standpoint the study has given the author insight into the methods and philosophy of church growth. We believe our churches have the finest Bible based doctrine in existence, but the majority of its churches are small because of a lack of church building methods. The aim of this study is to equip both church planters and pastors to do an effective job of starting new churches and leading existing ones to reach more people for Christ.

Methodology Utilized

Part of the material gained for this writing has come from the author's twenty-five years of ministry in the Free Will Baptist fellowship. Most of that time has been spent in home missions work either as a missionary, a board member, or a member of the Home Missions staff. In the last seven years, the author has visited all forty states where we have churches and conducted revivals and missionary services in those churches both new and old, large and small.

Hundreds of days each year have been spent in travel. By car, cassette tapes by great church builders have brought both inspiration and enlightenment. By airplane, books on church growth have been studied. For the past two years the courses from Luther Rice Seminary in preparation for the Master of Divinity degree have added to the research for this writing.

Finally, the actual research for the thesis has crystalized the truths gained from listening, observing, reading, and experimenting. From this background, the material has been compiled and put together.

Sources

Both primary and secondary sources have been utilized. The bibliography will reveal that approximately 150 works have been cited. These are listed as reference notes with direct citations in the writing. Most of the writings by successful church planters and builders of today were studied for reference. Some were referred to more than others, but all were helpful.

On the various subjects discussed in each chapter reference was made to books written on those particular subjects. These reference notes are included at the end of each chapter to make them readily available to the reader.

The serious student of the subject of church planting and growth will find the works cited in the bibliography helpful.

Organization of the Manuscript

The material is arranged in a step-by-step procedure for a man to settle in his heart the call from God to a particular city, then follow a plan in moving to that city. Next, the steps to take in beginning a fundamental church are discussed. How each phase of the church is to be organized is explained. Information on property and buildings is included.

The work is arranged so that a missionary can follow the guidelines in beginning, building, and leading his church to become indigenous. Information is included for the church to continue to grow until Christ returns.

The book is divided into thirteen chapters to allow for a study of one quarter if desired. Care was taken to make each chapter near the same length.

Each chapter contains headings of the topics discussed to

make it easy for the reader to find the section he desires to research. Both chapter titles and topics within each chapter are included in the Table of Contents.

A conclusion is placed at the end of each chapter so that each may stand as a separate unit. A brief conclusion to the entire manuscript is given at the end.

CHAPTER 1

WHY CHURCH PLANTING?

Church extension, the branching out into new communities for the purpose of establishing new churches that others may learn of Christ and His saving power, is greatly needed among fundamental denominations.[1] It is especially needed among fundamental churches for several reasons.

(1) Christ has commanded His people to be witnesses to their entire country, and we have not done it. One day we will meet God in judgment with the task unfinished.

(2) The country is decaying from within because of a lack of fundamental churches, and we could do something to turn this nation back to God.

(3) We will never have a strong missionary outreach around the world until a strong base at home is built.

(4) Our people are moving to many industrial cities of the country where there are no churches of their denomination. These people are almost all lost to the denomination, and many are lost to Christ.

(5) There are many lost, dying people in this nation, and we could reach many of them if more churches were organized.

The Scriptural Reason for Church Planting

The sending forth of workers with the gospel message within the boundaries of the sending country is included in the Great Commission,[2] Christ's final instructions to the Church. The first appearance of the Great Commission is Matthew 28:19, 20.

Go ye therefore, and teach all nations, baptizing
them in the name of the Father, and of the Son, and
of the Holy Ghost: Teaching them to observe all
things whatsoever I have commanded you: and, lo, I
am with you alway, even unto the end of the world.
Amen.

"All nations" includes America, but most fundamental
denominations have marshalled forces to reach the rest of the
world while leaving the reaching of America for Christ to
chance.[3]

The second appearance of the Great Commission is Mark
16:15, " . . . Go ye into all the world, and preach the gospel to
every creature." The words "every creature" include every
American. We are responsible for the people of this country.[4]
This includes the six million Jews (more than in Palestine),
twenty million Negroes (more than in many nations of Africa),
five million American Indians (of which only seven percent are
Protestant), five million Mexican Americans, and the seventy-
five million Catholics, Mormons, Buddhists, Mohammedans, and
other cults. More than one hundred million Americans have no
religious affiliation.[5]

In Luke 24:47 the Great Commission emphasizes the place
of beginning:

And that repentance and remission of sins should be
preached in his name among all nations, beginning at
Jerusalem.

This verse shows that all nations are to be reached, but the
place of beginning is Jerusalem, or the city where one lives.

Jesus is simply saying, "Start here," for these words were spoken to the apostles on the Mount of Olives at the edge of Jerusalem. Today, Palestine, where Jesus walked, where the Great Commission was given, and where the apostles preached, is a foreign mission field to all denominations because the early church did not see the constant need of evangelizing "Jerusalem." If the Lord tarries, America will become a "foreign mission field" unless fundamental, Bible-believing churches are planted in its cities to reach its inhabitants for Christ.[6]

Acts 1:8 outlines the program Christ gave for world evangelization:

> But ye shall receive power, after that the Holy Ghost is come upon you: and ye shall be witnesses unto me both in Jerusalem, and in all Judaea, and in Samaria, and unto the uttermost part of the earth.

The verse promises His power, outlines His program, and lists the places the church is to evangelize. Jerusalem, the first place mentioned, was the city where they were. So, the Great Commission does not begin in some remote outpost, but in one's own city. Acts 5:28 indicates they filled their city with their doctrine.[7] The words "in every house" of Acts 5:42 show that they did it by preaching and teaching both "in the temple" and "in every house" in their city.

It is to the American cities that church planters need to give particular attention. A hundred years ago ninety-five out of every one hundred Americans lived in the country. Today, three out of every four Americans live in the city.[8] This move to the industrial centers of the country has taken many families away from the church and caused them to be lost to the cause of

Christ. Those who move into new cities often do not establish themselves in a church because they cannot find one of their denomination, or one close to their doctrinal beliefs where they can feel comfortable. Moving has broken the regular habits of church attendance, they are not acquainted with anyone, no one is concerned about them, and they, like sheep, go astray.[9]

We need to plant churches in the cities because large numbers of our people have moved to cities where there are no churches of this denomination.[10] Many of the largest cities, most of the capital cities, the majority of the fast growing cities, and many towns of America have insufficient fundamental churches in them.

Most cities are in desperate need of Bible preaching churches. Suburbs have sprung up on the edge of every city. Churches have been built, but not nearly enough. Many churches in the inner cities have followed the example of the shopping centers and moved to the suburbs. Since then urban renewal programs have rebuilt the inner cities with apartment complexes and filled them with thousands of people who now live without a gospel preaching church within miles.[11]

Most of the population explosion is occurring in the urban areas. Because churches have failed to move to the cities, there are approximately nine times as many people alive today who are unevangelized than were alive when Jesus gave the Great Commission.[12]

After mentioning Jerusalem, Jesus used the words "all Judaea," in Acts 1:8. These words refer to the Roman province of Judea and would compare to one of the United States of America. Israel had three main sections, Judea, Samaria, and Galilee. Judea, the southern section, was where the gospel was first preached. The gospel quickly spread to the cities of that province. Acts 9:31 states, "Then had the churches rest throughout all Judaea . . . ."

We are strongest in twenty states. They are North Carolina, South Carolina, Georgia, Florida, Virginia, West Virginia, Ohio, Kentucky, Indiana, Illinois, Tennessee, Alabama, Mississippi, Arkansas, Missouri, Oklahoma, Kansas, Michigan, Texas, and California. These states would compare to Judea. Yet in each of these are found large cities and entire counties without the witness of our churches. The Scriptural command, " . . . be witnesses in all Judaea . . . ." applies here.

Next, Acts 1:8 mentions Samaria. As the word is used here it referred to the central division or province of Palestine. The only remaining section was that of Galilee.[13] So Palestine is a country of three states. The Book of Acts shows the early church filled the country of Palestine with churches. Acts 8:1 says, " . . . They were all scattered abroad throughout the regions of Judaea and Samaria . . . ." Acts 9:31 also states, "Then had the churches rest throughout all Judaea and Galilee and Samaria, and were edified . . . ."

The areas represented by Samaria and Galilee are those remaining thirty states not yet mentioned. Ten of those thirty states have no Free Will Baptist churches. They are North Dakota, South Dakota, Nebraska, Nevada, Utah, Wisconsin, New York, Connecticut, Vermont, and Rhode Island. Six of those thirty states, Wyoming, Hawaii, Montana, Minnesota, Delaware, and Massachusetts, have only one of our churches in the entire state. Fourteen of those thirty states have less than ten of our churches per state. They are Maine, New Hampshire, New Jersey, Pennsylvania, Maryland, Iowa, Louisiana, New Mexico, Arizona, Oregon, Washington, Idaho, Colorado, and Alaska.[14] In these thirty states are found millions of souls for whom Christ died that we need to evangelize.

The last area of the Great Commission given in Acts 1:8 is seen in the words "unto the uttermost part of the earth." In those days of the apostles these words represented all the world beyond the Palestinian borders.[15] To the church today they apply to the rest of the world outside the United States. The remaining part of the North American continent and all the other continents of the world are the evangelistic responsibility of the church.

After evangelizing its own country, the church sent missionaries to other areas. Paul, Barnabas, and John Mark were the first to be sent in this way. Acts 13:2, 3 states:

> As they ministered to the Lord, and fasted, the Holy Ghost said, Separate me Barnabas and Saul for the work whereunto I have called them. And when they had fasted and prayed, and laid their hands on them, they sent them away.

The plan outlined in the Book of Acts was to fill the homeland with churches to provide a base to send the gospel to the rest of the world. The foreign missions program can be no stronger than the home base that supports it. Jerusalem, all Judea, and Samaria must be filled with churches to give the men and money to take the gospel to the uttermost part of the earth. Unless a greater emphasis is given to home missions, there will be a gradual weakening in the foreign missions outreach.[16]

With the population shifting from rural to urban, churches are dying at the rate of one every hour. New churches must be started to replace those that die each year.[17] The Church of the Nazarene did a study of church growth from 1906 to 1971. They found that there was a close correlation between the number of churches planted and the growth of a denomination both at home and abroad. The study revealed that the growth of a denomination comes primarily by planting new congregations rather than strengthening existing churches.[18]

Unless new churches are begun in the cities of this country, the people will not be reached. If we fail here, we cannot advance on the foreign field because of lack of funds, personnel, and prayer.[19] Christ's cause can only be advanced as there are more and stronger churches at home. May we fill this land with our churches, not only to reach the masses of this country, but to provide a base to send the gospel to the uttermost part of the earth.

The Neglected Areas for Church Planting

First, a look at the various geographical sections of the country is necessary. The New England states are some of the most needy places in the entire country. This area is predominantly Catholic and has numerous towns and villages without a single gospel preaching church. Although the population in New England is increasing very little, one-fourth of the entire population of the United States lives east of Pennsylvania.

The Northeast is composed of the states of Maine, New Hampshire, Connecticut, Vermont, Rhode Island, New York, Pennsylvania, Maryland, New Jersey, Delaware, and Massachusetts.[20] At this writing we have less than twenty churches in all of this vast area.[21]

The second section to consider is the southern states. West Virgnina, Virginia, North Carolina, South Carolina, Kentucky, Tennessee, Alabama, Mississippi, Florida, Georgia, Louisiana, Arkansas, Texas, southern Missouri, and Oklahoma compose the section of the country known as the Bible Belt. This portion of the country is predominantly Baptist. It is also the stronghold for Methodists, Presbyterians, Nazarenes, and Pentecostals. The majority of our churches are found in these states.

The midwestern states of Michigan, Ohio, Indiana, Illinois, Wisconsin, Iowa, Minnesota, northern Missouri, Kansas, Nebraska, North Dakota, and South Dakota are primarily Lutheran with strong concentrations of Catholics.[22]

The mountain states are those states on either side of and including the Rocky Mountains. They are Colorado, Wyoming, Montana, Idaho, Utah, Nevada, Arizona, and New Mexico. These states, except southern Arizona, experience cold winters and deep snows. The spiritual temperature is cold also. Because of their location near Utah, all of these states have a large percentage of Mormons. The Catholic Church is very strong in these states also. A large number of the people in this section have no religious affiliation. However, some of the largest churches in the country are located in this area, such as Calvary Temple in Denver, Colorado. It is one of the top ten churches in the nation in attendance,[23] so, churches can be built in the cities of these states. We have only a few churches in this section.

The state of California is a conglomeration of just about everything religiously. It has the largest population of any state. It is also number one in rate of growth. We have about eighty churches in California.[24] A host of large cities without any of our churches can be found there.

The northwestern states of Washington and Oregon have the highest percentage of unchurched people of any section of the country. Most of the nine churches we have in these states were started by the National Home Missions Board.[25]

Alaska has a number of Baptist and Assembly of God churches and a large number of the cults. We have only two churches in Alaska, which were begun by the National Home Missions Board, and one missionary pilot who works in the Eskimo villages.

Hawaii has a heavy content of Buddhists, Catholics, and cults. We have one church there which is in the city of Waipahu. It was also established by the National Home Missions Board.

Canada is predominantly Anglican and Catholic religiously. We do not have a functioning church in Canada. Mexico is ninety-nine percent Catholic with only a sprinkling of fundamental churches. We have twelve churches and a school in Mexico, all products of the National Home Missions Board.

This concludes the look at the various sections of the country and the two other countries on the North American continent. A further look at particular places within those sections is necessary.

Three things should determine the need in a particular city. First, is the availability of the gospel. If there are an abundance of strong, aggressive, Bible-preaching, soul-winning churches in a city, that city would not be as needy as another without such churches.

Second to be considered, is the size of the city. One should not put precious time into a small out of the way place and overlook the large metropolitan areas where large members can be reached with the gospel. The small places should be reached, but they are not the places to start. The Biblical principle of Paul was to establish churches in the large cities of Philippi, Athens, Corinth, and Ephesus, and then challenge those churches to extend the gospel to the regions beyond them.

Third, to be considered, is the rate of growth of a city. If the town is dying and people are moving away, it would be better to establish churches in the places where the people are going rather than those places they are leaving.

We need to plant churches in the Northeast. New York City is a great need because of its tremendous population and because of the fact that Bible-preaching, soul-winning churches are so scarce. Dr. Max Helton, a Baptist authority on church planting, believes New York City to be the most needy place in the world. The city and surrounding areas have more than sixteen million people. The area does not have a single aggressive Bible-preaching, soul-winning church averaging 400 in Sunday school. The mayor of New York City is one of the most influential men in the nation. When one considers the commercial trade, the foreigners who receive their first impression of America there, the ghettos, the headlines of crime, the gangs, the business people, and factory workers whose lives could be changed by the preaching of the gospel by faithful, spirit-filled preachers, our church planters need to look toward New York City.

Boston is the second most needy city in New England because more people live in Boston than in all the states of Maine, Connecticut, New Hampshire, and the rest of Massachusetts combined.[26] Any city one would choose in the northeastern section needs a Free Will Baptist church because of the scarcity of the gospel in that section of the country.

Next the state of California should be given priority by our church planters because of the large cities already there and the exploding population of the state.

Fourth, the sun states of Arizona, Texas, and Florida should receive emphasis because they are growing so rapidly. Each of these states has numerous cities where we have no churches and an insufficient amount of Bible-preaching churches to reach the people.

The cities of the states in the southern section are the least needy in the country because they have the largest concentration of our churches and Bible-preaching churches of other denominations. But the most needy city in this section is New Orleans, Louisiana.

The midwestern states have a number of large cities such as Chicago, Illinois; Milwaukee, Wisconsin; Minneapolis, Minnesota; Omaha, Nebraska; Minot, North Dakota; and hundreds of other cities which are needy places.

In the mountain states, the cities of Pueblo, Colorado Springs, and Grand Junction, Colorado; Cheyenne, Casper, Rock Springs, Laramie, and Rawlins, Wyoming; Great Falls, Helena, and Kalispell, Montana are needy. Nevada's cities of Reno and Las Vegas would compare to Sodom and Gomorrah of the Bible because of their sins. Nevada also has a number of small towns without a church of any kind. Some of the people in the small mountain villages of the Rockies, such as State Bridge, Colorado and dozens of other towns, would have to drive in excess of one hundred miles to find a gospel-preaching church.

Utah's Salt Lake City, Ogden, Provo, and Moab are desperately in need of the gospel. In New Mexico the cities of Albuquerque, Santa Fe, Las Cruces, and Alamogordo should be considered.

The Phoenix, Arizona area with suburbs of Tempe, Mesa, and Scottsdale are some of the places with mushrooming populations because of climate, industry, and living conditions.

Idaho is the native state of this writer who was saved in the First Free Will Baptist church begun in the northwestern states.

This is a vivid testimony of the fruits of launching out into new territory. Idaho Falls, Coeur d' Alene, Moscow, Nampa, and Caldwell are some cities in Idaho that need Free Will Baptist churches.

In Oregon, Huntington, Pendleton, La Grande, Bend, and Eugene are needy cities, as well as Bellevue, Olympia, Walla Walla, Spokane, and Pasco in Washington.

The list is endless. Huge cities in every state, Canada, and Mexico are an evangelistic challenge we need to accept. For further information on needy cities contact the National Home Missions Department. They publish a list of capital cities, their population and needs, a list of one hundred forty cities without any of our churches, a list of the fifty most needy cities, and a list of the ten fastest growing cities in America.

Conclusion

The need is not more places to go, but preachers with a pioneering spirit. The church planter must let God burn an indelible impression of a city on his soul and move to that city to plant an aggressive soul-winning church.

The church planter must go into this work fully prepared. Without the necessary training and experience, he will flounder and become discouraged. This could cause him to give up and leave in defeat. Such defeat leaves its impression on the city. It leaves its mark on the man and it is discouraging to his supporters.

Men who will adequately prepare, and lay the proper foundation under the work of church planting, will find it a joyous and rewarding labor for the Lord. Church planting can be the most thrilling work one can experience in the ministry if there is a call from God, proper preparation, and a burden for the work.

Chapter 1
Reference Notes

[1]Charles W. H. Scott and others, *The Modern Pioneer* (Springfield, Missouri: Assemblies of God Home Missions Department, 1967), p. 5.

[2]Peter F. Gunther, *The Fields at Home* (Chicago: Moody Press, 1963), p. 10. Used by permission.

[3]John V. Ohlin, "A Church Is Born," *Church Growth America* (September/October, 1976), p. 12.

[4]*Ibid.*

[5]Homer E. Willis, *Why Home Missions* (Nashville: Free Will Baptist Home Missions Board, 1969), pp. 1-6.

[6]Lyle Wacker and others, *Church Extension Handbook* (Forest Park, Illinois: North American Baptist Missionary Society, n.d.), p. 3.

[7]Roy Thomas, *Missions on the Move* (Nashville: Free Will Baptist Home Missions Board, 1978), p. 3.

[8]Willis, pp. 1-6.

[9]Wacker, p. 3.

[10]Gunther, p. 17.

[11]Roy Thomas, *The Hunger in North America* (Nashville: Free Will Baptist Home Missions Board, 1974), p. 5.

[12]William A. Powell, *The Urban Church Survey Manual* (Atlanta: Home Mission Board, Southern Baptist Convention, 1972), p. 20.

[13]Albert Barnes, *Barnes' Notes on the New Testament, Acts* (Grand Rapids: Baker Book House, 1956), p. 6.

[14]*Directory of Free Will Baptist Churches* (Nashville: Free Will Baptist Executive Department, 1977), p. 9 *et. passim.*

[15]Barnes, p. 6.

[16]Gunther, p. 9.

[17]Wacker, p. 3.

[18]Win Arn and David McGavran, "Planned Parenthood," *Church Growth America* (September/October, 1976), p. 7.

[19]Wacker, p. 3.

[20]*Rand McNally Road Atlas* (Chicago: Rand McNally and Company, 1976), p. 5.

[21]*Directory of Free Will Baptist Churches,* p. 62.

[22]Max Helton, "Where to Go," (Hammond, Indiana: Helton Publications, n.d.).

[23]Elmer Towns, *America's Fastest Growing Churches* (Nashville: Impact Books, 1972), p. 11.

[24]*Directory of Free Will Baptist Churches,* pp. 24-27.

[25]Max Helton, "Where to Go."

[26]*Ibid.*

CHAPTER II

THE PASTOR

Competent pastoral leadership is the first requirement in the building of a church.[1] A church is always built by a man, but never on a man. Those who start churches must be motivated by God who is its founder, and be driven by the impossible dream to accomplish the unperformable task.[2]

The Call, Burden, and Vision of the Church Planter

The man who starts a church must be called of God. This call involves a burden to win souls, a desire to preach, and a compulsion that he cannot do anything else in life. He must surrender himself to God, prepare himself for service, prove himself to those who will ordain him, test his ideas in an established local church, and then move to the city God lays on his heart to begin the church.[3]

How does one determine God's call? First, he should carefully examine his own motives. Money should not be a factor.[4] Two wrong possibilities exist. First, one might be employed by a mission board in order to receive a substantial raise in pay. Second, moving to a city where there is no existing church may involve financial insecurity. However, if the preacher is where God wants him, He will take care of him financially.

The fact that no existing church wants to call him for pastor does not constitute a call to start a church.[5] A desire to be like someone else who has been successful is not a reason for starting a church. The climate in an area, the recreation or business opportunities, or the fact that it is close to home should not be the determining factors in starting a church in a given place. The church planter is not looking around for a place to better himself, but he is looking to God so that he can better his place.[6]

The fact that one sees a need does not by itself constitute a call. There are needs everywhere. A man can be in only one place at a time. He must determine through an abiding, compelling conviction, coupled with much prayer and waiting before God, that this is the perfect will of God for his life.

A part of determining God's call to plant a church must include a look at one's own qualifications. Although it is natural to feel unequipped and unprepared, a church planter needs to take a candid look at himself and his family before he undertakes the task of going to a city to begin a church.

The most obvious beginning place is that of the physical health of the church planter and his wife. He needs to be able to spend long hours in visitation and have the physical stamina to "swing a hammer." The man who cracks under a 60-hour week. is not physically strong enough to start a church.[7]

Both he and his wife need mental and emotional stability. They should be people who are not easily discouraged and do not become dissatisfied when the "new" has worn off. They should not be people who are fraught with worries and nerve problems.

The entire family should agree that this is God's will. A wife and children can cause real problems if they are grudgingly moved to a new city where unwanted sacrifices and demands are placed upon them. The family should pray together about the matter until they realize that God is leading in this direction.[8]

He must be the kind of man who does not have to be told what to do. The church planter does not punch a time clock. No one in his congregation will be able to outline his schedule. No one will check to see if he sleeps late. He can give the illusion of being very busy and working long hours while a day's work is not really done.[9] He can spend his time on things that do not profit. Keeping up with the urgent can create a constant pressure which stops any significant attention to what is really important. He will have to go on his own initiative, encourage himself in the Lord when things don't go well, and keep on regardless of setbacks, determined to see the job completed.[10] He must not be lazy.

He should possess a pioneer spirit which will enable him to improvise and get the job done when there are insufficient funds and personnel. Men who start churches will need to swing a hammer and negotiate a loan, promote in the pulpit and advertise in the newspaper, preach, counsel, teach and train. He must be quick to acquire knowledge in a hundred areas where he is uninformed. He must lead authoritatively, for no one in the congregation knows how to build a church. He must be equipped with deep commitment, iron will, wide scholarship, and vast experience. He must be able to do it all, for in the beginning he will have little or no help.[11]

He should be humble. He will minister to a small group in inadequate facilities, with insufficient help in the beginning.[12]

He should be socially and educationally acceptable to the people he seeks to win. He needs an outgoing personality and a love for people that will enable him to meet them. He should be sincerely interested in their problems and have a genuine desire to help them.[13]

He must be a soul-winner. The person who is afraid or unwilling to visit alone, who cannot come to grips with people about their souls and present the gospel on a one-to-one basis, is not the kind of man needed as a church planter.[14]

He should be a mature Christian with a thorough knowledge of the Bible and church administration. He should know how to organize, train, inspire, and put people to work.[15] Both he and his family should be separated from the world and dedicated to God with devotional lives that will keep them close to the Lord.

He should be an ordained preacher and thoroughly convinced of his doctrines so that he can teach them to others. The man who is too ashamed, too afraid, or too weak to teach his doctrine will not succeed as a church planter.[16]

He needs some knowledge of the procedure of building a church plant. He should know methods of financing, building codes, and legal requirements for church buildings.[17]

He also needs a knowledge of church planting and church growth methods. He must be totally convinced of the philosophy of a soul-winning, aggressive church.

He must be prepared to sacrifice. He should know how to handle money and have practiced sacrificial living, which, though unpopular today, is a must in new church work. He should not be burdened down with debts and should learn to live within his means so as not to ruin his influence by having overdue bills.

After reading this list of qualifications one might ask, "Who can start a church?" The answer lies not in age, nor experience, nor in education, but in the call of God and in strategy, which is a preconceived plan of action.[18]

These qualifications should not scare off good men whom God would have to plant a church, but they should serve to show that the work is difficult and will call for the very best from the preacher and his family.

Another part of a call to begin a church is the leadership of the Holy Spirit to a certain city. The preacher should make sure about the will of the Lord in the choice of a city. He will need to know that the Lord led him there when the winds of adversity begin to blow. It could make the difference between success and failure.[19] The Lord may use a number of things to impress the place upon the heart of the preacher. There may be a nucleus of people asking for a preacher to come. The fact that the city does not have one of our churches might challenge him. A mission board might approach him about a city, or he might visit a particular city and the Lord speak to his heart about it.[20]

God is able to let the preacher know the place He would have him go. He will lay it on his heart until it becomes an abiding conviction that this is the will of God. The preacher will fall in love with that city.[21]

He may test God's leadership by visiting the city. It should be a good sized, growing place, and as he views the city he should begin to come up with a plan of action to be used in beginning a church there.[22] He should see the people lost without Christ as he drives through the streets. He might get on a hill outside of town and let God burn a burden for that city into his soul and leave saying as Paul said at Ephesus, " . . . I will return again unto you, if God will . . . " (Acts 18:21).

Biblical Pastoral Leadership

A most important factor in beginning a church is its

conception in the mind of the church planter who is motivated by the Holy Spirit. The church must be large in the heart of the pastor before it will ever be large on the street corner.[23] It is important that the pastor get a vision of building a strong church, for the church will never rise above the pastor's leadership, and the pastor will never lead the church further than his own vision.

The definition of an ideal pastor is a preacher who has found adequacy in Christ that enables him to relate to others in his home, church, or outside world. He has developed skills in communicating the gospel. He believes in long pastorates and sees himself in the very place God wants him. He is disciplined in time management, study habits, and personal finance. He is able to live happily in the denominational framework and still feel the freedom of personal expression and professional fulfillment. His life is dominated by love and purity.[24]

The Biblical role of pastoral leadership leads to several Scriptures. The words "bishop" and "elder" are used interchangeably in the Bible (Titus 1:5-7) and refer to the office of pastor. The word "elder" denotes seniority (1 Peter 5:5). This means he is to be a mature Christian worthy of the respect of the flock. He is to be an ensample or example to the flock (1 Peter 5:3). He is to take the oversight (1 Peter 5:2) which means to oversee (Acts 20:28). He is to administer rule over the church (1 Timothy 5:17). The Bible exhorts church members in the following verses:

> " . . . Know them which labor among you, and are over you in the Lord, and admonish you; And to esteem them very highly in love for their work's sake. And be at peace among yourselves" (1 Thess. 5:12, 13).

"Remember them which have the rule over you, who have spoken unto you the word of God: whose faith follow, considering the end of their conversation" (Hebrews 13:7).

"Obey them that have the rule over you, and submit yourselves: for they watch for your souls, as they that must give account, that they may do it with joy, and not with grief: for that is unprofitable for you" (Hebrews 13:17).

These verses do not refer to a dictator. The pastor who must *demand* allegiance reveals his lack of maturity. The Biblical pastor gets cooperation first by example, and second by the Scriptural office he holds.[25]

The word "bishop" means overseer or superintendent. The word "elder" implies the pastor's personal qualifications, and the word "bishop" suggests his duties.

First Timothy 3:1 says, "This is a true saying, If a man desire the office of a bishop, he desireth a good work." Work is exactly what the pastorate is.[26] The pastor is to rule his own house, " . . . For if a man know not how to rule his own house, how shall he take care of the house of God?" (1 Tim. 3:5). The pastor is to rule the church as he rules his home.

The Scriptural plan is as follows: The pastor is the leader, the deacons give support to the pastor in carrying out the ministry, and the congregation is the final seat of authority to determine policy, direction, and discipline. This gives the church a threefold system of checks and balances. The pastor, the deacons, and the congregation each depend on the other while mutually supporting one another in the Biblical task before them.[27]

If a church is to be built, there must be positive leadership at the top.[28] Competent pastoral leadership is the first answer to the problem of building a church. The Holy Spirit will enable a pastor to become a leader if he will submit himself to Him.[29]

Almost without exception, the lack of success means the lack of effective leadership. Leadership is the key to church growth. The church planter must think ahead, plan for the future, envision problems, and come up with solutions to them. When he gets the answer he must communicate these answers to his people. A leader draws his inspiration from future projections and not from past accomplishments.[30]

It is important that the church planter be fully convinced that God has chosen him as the leader of the church. The leader of the church is not the denominational executives, the heads of the Bible colleges, the official board of the local church, the deacon board, or the local congregation.[31]

It is God's will for the pastor to be the leader of the church. There is yet to be a church with a system of congregational government leadership control that is really moving ahead with fantastic success. Any dynamic, progressive, and enthusiastic pastor will find his style being cramped, his energies draining away, and his dreams turning to despair if he has to sell his plans and dreams to a negative thinking congregation.[32]

The leadership of the church rests in the hands of a full-time executive who is paid a full-time salary to think and plan ahead and lead the church on to victory. No one can do this but the pastor. The Bible is crystal clear. The pastor is God's appointed leader of the church.

Several things show this to be true. Leadership is full-time. No layman, deacon, or church board can give full-time leadership. Only the pastor can. Leadership carries with it responsibility. It must be assumed by someone who can give the church first place in his life. Only the man God has called and put there can do that. Leadership is thinking big. The pastor should be the man with the greatest faith and the largest vision and the fondest dreams in the church. Leadership is organization. An organization cannot function without a head and it can only have one head. It must be the pastor. Leadership is leading. The pastor must determine the direction God is leading, and then inspire the people to follow him in that direction.[33]

Leadership of the church is to be in the hands of a man who is constantly thinking, constantly praying, constantly reaching out, and constantly surrendering himself to the Holy Spirit. That can only be the pastor.[34]

The church planter must settle it in his mind at the outset that he is going to be the leader of the church. If the church is begun with Biblical pastoral leadership, God will bless and the church will grow. The church is not to lead the pastor, but the pastor is to lead the church. A study made in 1969 of the ten largest Sunday schools in America revealed that they all had certain things in common. They were all conservative and evangelistic. They all preached and believed the Bible was true. They all minimized activity and majored on outreach. They all had a pastor in whom the people had entrusted great leadership.[35]

The church planter must assume the leadership in the beginning. Not everything should be voted on. Things that are right to do, such as receiving an offering or praying, should not be voted on. Just do them. Things that are wrong, such as sponsoring a dance, should not be voted on. Just do not do them. Every dime spent should not be voted on. Instead, the church should adopt a budget that is planned carefully and prayerfully, and then confine the spending to that which is within the budget.[36]

This is not to suggest that the pastor is a dictator. Dictators rule by force while pastors lead in love. It will be well for the church planter to remember that political dictators usually have wrong motives in mind and eventually drive the people to their only resource of rebellion which results in a revolution and ends in the assassination of the dictator.

Let not the church planter fear to take the lead in the church lest he become a dictator. The pastor is not a dictator if he is a strong leader because he is hired by vote of the congregation. He reports to the church board and to the congregation and they have a right to overrule his recommendations. He appoints committees, but the church gives him the authority and the board approves the appointments. The pastor can only recommend and launch a project. The success of any program can only be effected by loyal laymen who pick up the ideas of their leader and make them work.[37]

But the church planter must remember that leadership begins with example. If the pastor is a soul-winner, others will follow his example. A home-going pastor makes church-going people. When the pastor begins bringing converts down the aisle, he will be able to lead his people in soul-winning. Dr. R. G. Lee at Bellevue Baptist Church in Memphis, Tennessee averaged ten visits per day for a ten-year period.[38] The church planter who will get out and visit and win souls will build a church. The fellow who does not visit will fail.

The Pastor's Schedule

The pastor's responsibilities are many and the job is a

big one. He is expected to study and prepare so that he can preach good, fresh sermons at every service. He is to be equipped to teach the church so the people will be prepared to do their jobs. He must visit the sick, shut-ins, and absentees. He must also have some time for personal soul-winning. The administrative duties of the church will demand part of his time. There will be people to counsel. He will have to take the lead in building programs. All the new converts will require follow up. His family must have some attention.

This list of demands upon the preacher may overwhelm him. He may work himself into a frenzy and yet always feel inadequate in each area of his responsibility. In despair he may give up and become lazy.

The pastorate presents the best opportunity for laziness of almost any position. There is no clock for the preacher to punch. If he has working hours, he arranges them to suit himself. The preacher's conscience and his God are the only actual checks on his time.

He can neglect the work of the church he now pastors by building air castles of the dream church he hopes to pastor. A minister's varied duties permit an unlimited exercise of liberty which may stimulate ministerial laziness. If he is not seen doing one thing, he could be doing another. If he is not out visiting, he could be at the church in conference. If he is not at the church or out visiting, he could be at home studying. He could be making his rounds at the hospitals. He could even be out of town on denominational business.[39]

An apparent lack of appreciation on the part of the people may cause a pastor to be lax in his work. Another contributing cause of ministerial laziness is a lack of plans. A man has no choice but to be lazy if he doesn't know where to begin, how to proceed, and when to stop. But laziness will result in a short pastorate, an undisturbed baptistry, and a dwindling congregation.[40]

For these reasons the pastor needs a schedule. The following is a sample schedule which could be adopted to any pastorate:

PASTOR'S SAMPLE DAILY SCHEDULE

7:00 A.M.   *Rise, shower, get dressed.* (Look nice.)
             Eat a good breakfast. (Guard your health.)

8:00 to 11:30   *Go to office.*
                 Study Bible. (Study one book in the Bible.)
                 Spend time in prayer.
                 Work on sermons.
                 Work on Sunday school and Church Training lessons.
                 Work on prayer meeting message.
                 Read from a good book.
                 Work on activities listed in church calendar.
                 Plan promotion, advertising, programs.
                 Write promotional letters.
                 Answer all correspondence.

12:00   *Eat lunch.*

1:00 P.M.   *Go on visitation.*
             1. Visit new attenders to church.
             2. Visit prospects.
             3. Visit absentees. (Train teachers to do this.)

               4. Visit hospitals.

               5. One afternoon a week knock on new doors.

4:00   *Spend time with family.*

               1. Spend time with children.

               2. Mow yard, work in garden, or relax.

               3. Eat dinner.

7:00   *Go soul-winning.*

9:00   *Relax with family.*

An explanation of this schedule will shed some light on it. The pastor should get up in the morning and prepare to go to work the way all other workers do. It is a shame for a preacher to lie in bed after his church members have gone to work and his children have gone to school.

He should bathe every morning, shave, and get fully dressed. A preacher is in a class with professional men, even though many times he may not have the money for clothes the professional man has. However, he needs to be clean and neat, with his shoes shined, a clean shirt, and a freshly pressed suit. He should look his very best everyday because he, above all others, represents Christ and the church. People who look successful in their dress receive preferential treatment in almost all of their social or business encounters. The reason some men do not dress in a manner that commands respect is not lack of money, but lack of knowledge of style and quality in clothing. The average man can easily create the look of success by choosing his clothes properly.[41]

The pastor should be careful about his hair. A fundamentalist should wear a short, clean-cut hairstyle at all times. The length of a man's hair can keep him from being widely used in Bible-believing churches if it becomes long or shaggy looking.

The pastor should eat a good breakfast and do all he can to take care of his health. If a man is in vigorous health, there is life to his step and vitality in his manner. The vigor of his healthy body has in a miraculous way encouraged a vitality of spirit which increases his total liveliness.[42] Heart attacks and nervous breakdowns are sometimes the payoff for preachers who fail to take care of their bodies. The pastor should provide for himself some sort of suitable exercise. Without it he will become sluggish and unfit for his best work. Many times when the pastor feels depressed and his work becomes irksome, he will gain a new perspective if he will get away from it and engage in some kind of physical exercise.[43]

He will not have an office at the church in the beginning. So his office will have to be in his home. If possible, he should have a separate room for his office. If such a room is not available he can have a desk and bookcase in one room which will distinguish that room as his office.[44]

The mornings should generally be given to study and prayer with one exception. People are usually taken to surgery early in the morning. The pastor will want to be there to share Scripture and prayer with the patient before he is taken from the hospital room to surgery. Sometimes the pastor can visit other hospital patients while he is at the hospital early in the morning.[45]

In the study the pastor should constantly be giving intensive study to at least one book in the Bible. The preacher who does this will have a good working knowledge of the entire Bible in a few years.

His prayer life should be meaningful. There should be specific things for which he is praying. The following is a general list which could be followed:

On *Monday*, pray for the various *missionaries*.
On *Tuesday*, pray for the *task* God has given him and others.
Wednesday could be the day to pray especially for *workers* both in the church and around the world.
Thursday is a good day for *thanksgiving*.
On *Friday*, pray for the *families* and *finances*.
Saturday, remember the *saints*.
Sunday, pray for the *services* and *sinners*.

The preparation of next Sunday's sermons should begin on Monday. This gives God the opportunity to burn the message into the preacher's heart and gives the preacher a thousand opportunities to gather fresh, real life illustrations during the week.

The Bible says, " . . . Give attendance to reading . . . " (1 Tim. 4:13). The pastor should have a good book he is reading all the time, such as biographies of great preachers or books on church growth. Pastor Jim McAllister suggests that the preacher should read three books per week. This will add continually many good books to the preacher's library and also keep him abreast of new developments in church growth methods. He should also subscribe to publications that will keep him informed about what is happening in the world about him, as well as publications which will give him new ideas for sermons and promotion of the work of the church.

There will be more said about the church calendar later, but the pastor should plan well the services and activities the church will conduct. He should spend some time planning his promotions and advertisement.

Correspondence should be answered promptly, especially where it relates to church business. Many times pastors are dilatory in getting letters out to church visitors, newcomers to the community, and other prospects, thus losing opportunities to reach these people for the church and Christ.

In planting a new church, a great deal of time must be spent in visitation. Everyone who attends church for the first time should be visited the following week without fail. All the time possible needs to be spent knocking on new doors, but at least one afternoon per week should be reserved for it.

Some time must be spent with the family. The preacher can spend about three hours around supper time relaxing with his family, then make some soul-winning calls and return home in time to have prayer and family devotions with the children before they go to bed. Then he and his wife can visit, read, and relax before retiring.

Of course, the preacher cannot perform the same tasks every day. So a weekly schedule is necessary also. The following is a suggested weekly schedule for the pastor:

Monday should be a light day. The preacher might relax around the house, perform tasks around the house, or set some time on this day for recreation such as fishing. If he works, he could come in early and spend some time at home and perhaps take the family out to eat.

Tuesday morning should be spent in the office and Tuesday afternoon visiting and contacting absentees.

Wednesday morning he will want to get ready for prayer

meeting and work on the sermons for Sunday. Wednesday afternoon he should visit.

Thursday morning he will need to plan his church visitation for that night and also send out his daytime visitors. Thursday afternoon would be a good time to reserve for knocking on new doors.

Friday morning he should complete his preparations for Sunday and spend Friday afternoon soul-winning.

Saturday morning he should meet with his bus workers for prayer and instruction before they go out to visit. Then he could spend some time at home, make calls from about 11:00 until 1:00, and come home and do something special with the family. Saturday night should be spent relaxing with some time in prayer for the next day.

Sunday morning he should go to the church early and be alone with the Lord. After the morning services he should rest, study, and pray for the evening services.[46]

The pastor who goes into a town to plant a church also needs a long range schedule. He needs to take a vacation before he goes to the new city, and not take any more vacations or revival meetings for that year so that he can spend that entire year in getting the new church on its feet.

The preacher who gets a lot done will do it on purpose. He must plan his work and work his plan. If interruptions get him off schedule, he should return to it as soon as possible. He must learn to not let people monopolize or waste his time, and yet remain available and approachable for counseling and other appointments. Whether the suggested schedule is used or not, the pastor who has a schedule and goes by it will succeed in his work.

The Pastor's Family

The church planter's family will undergo a great deal for the sake of his calling. They will move to a city where they are strangers. Their church, at least at first, will have few with which to fellowship. The facilities will be far from ideal. Starting a new church means the pastor's family will not have him around the house very much, especially in the beginning when many hours of foundational door knocking is being done.

The pastor does not have to sacrifice his family in order to start a church. First, before the endeavor is undertaken, it should be settled among all members of the family that this is the will of God for their lives. That makes it a family project, which can be the most thrilling experience a family can have together in a lifetime.

The pastor must work at the job of having a secure, happy, contented family. So many are losing their children, and an alarming number of preachers and their wives are separating. Having a happy family life will make the pastor more successful. If the pastor loses the battle on the home front, he will lose it everywhere else.

Planting and growing a church should bring the family closer together. The pastor should have no close personal friends in the church because he cannot show partiality. This should draw him closer to his family. The pastor's wife will be unable to have close personal friends in the church lest it create jealousy, so she will need a close relationship with her husband and children.

The pastor's children many times may be ostracized and laughed at, especially if they attend public schools, because of their convictions and doctrines. They will need the security of a happy home where they can come as a refuge from the storms of life.

One of the greatest needs in America is the home to be established on Biblical principles. The pastor will have little success in dealing with other families' problems if his own house is not in order. The   father is to be the *head* of the home, the wife is to be the *heart* of the home, the children are to be the *hub* of the home, and Christ is to be the *hope* of the home.[47]

The church planter should buy a house as soon as possible when he goes to a new city. This will give security to both the family and the church, because it clearly shows that the preacher intends to stay and do a work for God in that city. It will also help with deductions on his income tax, and enable him to accumulate an equity which he may need in later years.

It should not be an expensive home with high payments, but a comfortable nice looking home that he can afford. The home and yard should be well kept at all times. It is a terrible testimony to the community when the preacher's home and yard are poorly kept. On the other hand, he should not get so involved with flowers, shrubs, and garden that he has no time to build a church.

Of course, the main things about a home is not the house, but the people who live there. The pastor must remember that he is also a father and the pastor to his wife and family. He should plan his schedule so that he can spend time with his family. The family should eat together, play together, go to church together, and pray together. The pastor will have to say "no" to other people in some instances, but he should not cancel family appointments to do things with other people.

Many preachers do not take a vacation, and if they do, they use the time to conduct a revival meeting. This writer believes that is a mistake. The pastor needs a vacation and so does his family. If a man does his job all year, there is nothing unscriptural about taking a vacation with his family.[48]

Another important lesson the pastor must learn is that of not letting church problems make him hard to live with and unpleasant. Children can be turned sour on the church and its people because of what they hear around the table and in the home. Some men maintain their composure in public, but in the privacy of the home take their frustrations out on the family. If a man destroys the confidence of his children in his Christianity, he will pay dearly in heartache and tears. He must learn to take problem situations and problem people to the Lord, and when he comes home, come in with victory in his soul and joy in his heart.

The pastor and his wife need to work at staying in love. It is wholesome for the pastor's children and his church to know that he and his wife love each other.[49] They should not argue or criticize each other in public. They need to guard their own hearts constantly so that the devil cannot put lust for another in place of their love for each other. Too many brokenhearted companions, children, and churches show the terrible effects of a preacher or his wife who let this happen.

The pastor should see that his children are trained. This training should cover four areas.

First, they should be trained in *spiritual* things. They should learn the Bible, how to behave in church, how to accept Christ as Savior, how to pay their tithes, how to win souls and serve God.

Second, they should be trained *physically.* Every child should learn to work. There was work before sin entered the world and there will be work in Heaven. The person who does not learn to work will miss much of life's blessings. The children should be trained to take care of their bodies so as to be clean and conserve their health.

Third, the children should be trained *mentally*. Their minds should be developed with good education. Pastors should instill in the minds of their children to do the best they can in school. The person who just barely gets by in school will be that way in his work when he grows up. Children should be taught an appreciation of good music, art, and literature, and also to participate in these cultural activities.

Fourth, children should be trained *socially*. The pastor's children should not demonstrate his failure in this area by having poor manners or appearance. They should be taught to respect their elders and to get along with other children. They should be taught good table manners, good telephone manners, and the social graces.

Another family area the pastor needs to be very cautious in is that of finanical matters. The pastor should learn to live within his means. Debts and women have destroyed more ministers than anything else. Pastors should pay as they go. This is not to say that they should never go in debt, for few would ever have a house or a car without debts. But debts should be watched so there will not be "a lot of month left at the end of the money." The lay-away plan is a better plan than the installment plan. Neither preachers, nor their families ought to complain about financial matters. They should manage what they receive and trust the Lord to meet their needs.[50] For the pastor or his wife to "poor mouth" and complain to members of the congregation about their financial problems is to cause loss of confidence in the pastor's finanical leadership ability.

The minister's family should be faithful to the church

services and take part in all that the church does. His wife should go on visitation as other women in the church are expected to do. She should not be expected to be the assistant pastor, but just a faithful Christian as all other women in the congregation.[51]

The pastor's family should set examples for the congregation in standards of dress and behavior. His wife and children should share his convictions and back what he preaches from the pulpit by the lives they live. They should be separated from the world and have a compassion for lost sinners that would be examples for others in the congregation to follow.

Being a pastor is a huge responsibility which involves the entire family. But the man who determines to be a good pastor will have a happy, well adjusted family, and will rejoice in doing the most necessary and gratifying work in life.

Conclusion

The pastor must find joy and contentment in the ministry. If the work is a drudgery to him, his discontentment will come out in his sermons, his counseling, and all that he does. That which he does to attract people will drive them away.

The pastor's attitude toward the ministry will have much to do with the happiness of his wife and family also. They will find joy in the work of the Lord if he does. A contented family will do much to inspire confidence and cause people to come to church and to Christ.

Much has been said about leadership in this chapter. The key to successful leadership is love. If the pastor has genuine love for his church, his people, and his family, they will gladly follow his leadership. Consequently, he will never disappoint their confidence by carelessly leading them in the wrong direction.

Chapter II
Reference Notes

[1]Leslie Parrot, *Building Today's Church* (Grand Rapids: Baker Book House, 1973), p. 36.

[2]Elmer Towns, *Getting a Church Started in the Face of Insurmountable Odds with Limited Resources in Unlikely Circumstances* (Nashville: Impact Books, 1975), p. 11.

[3]*Ibid.*, p. 150.

[4]Roy Thomas, *How to Start a Church from Scratch* (Nashville: Free Will Baptist Board of Home Missions, 1974), p. 2.

[5]*Ibid.*

[6]Lee Lebsack, *Ten at the Top* (Stow, Ohio: New Hope Press, 1974) p. 20.

[7]Towns, p. 14.

[8]*Ibid.*

[9]Thomas, p. 2.

[10]Parrot, p. 27.

[11]Towns, p. 17.

[12]*Ibid.*

[13]Melvin L. Hodges, *A Guide to Church Planting* (Chicago: Moody Press, 1973), p. 28. Used by permission.

[14]Win Arn and Donald McGavran, "Planned Parenthood," *Church Growth America* (September/October, 1976), p. 7.

[15]Grant C. Rice, *Principles of New Church Planting* (Rockvale, Tennessee: Grant C. Rice Church Planting—

Consulting, 1977), p. 2.

[16]Thomas, p. 2.

[17]*Ibid.*

[18]Rice, p. 2.

[19]Towns, p. 130.

[20]Thomas, p. 3.

[21]Max Helton, "Where to Go," (Hammond, Indiana: Helton Publications, n.d.).

[22]*Ibid.*

[23]Towns, p. 129.

[24]Parrot, p. 223.

[25]Towns, p. 171.

[26]*Ibid.*

[27]Towns, p. 174.

[28]Lebsack, p. 19.

[29]Parrot, p. 36.

[30]Robert Schuller, *Your Church Has Real Possibilities* (Glendale, California: Regal Books, 1974), p. 49. Used by permission.

[31]*Ibid.*, pp. 50-51.

[32]*Ibid.*, p. 53.

[33]*Ibid.*, p. 57.

[34]*Ibid.*, p. 58.

[35]John Bisagno, *How to Build an Evangelistic Church* (Nashville: Broadman Press, 1972), p. 17. Used by permission.

[36]*Ibid.*, p. 18.

[37]Schuller, p. 56.

[38]George Godfrey, *Helps to Have a Soul Winning Church* (Crown Point, Indiana: Hyles-Anderson College, 1976), p. 39.

[39]Adolph Bedsole, *The Pastor in Profile* (Grand Rapids: Baker Book House, 1958), p. 77.

[40]*Ibid.*, p. 79.

[41]John T. Molloy, *Dress for Success* (New York, New York: Warner Communications, 1975),p. 12. Used by permission.

[42]Aubrey P. Andelin, *Man of Steel and Velvet* (Santa Barbara, California: Pacific Press, 1977), p. 221.

[43]Howard F. Snyden and Warren W. Wiersbe, *When the Pastor Wonders How* (Chicago: Moody Press, 1973), p. 146. Used by permission.

[44]Jack Hyles, *Let's Build an Evangelistic Church* (Murfreesboro, Tennessee: Sword of the Lord Publishers, 1962), p. 116.

[45]Homer A. Kent, Sr., *The Pastor and His Work* (Chicago: Moody Press, 1963), p. 18. Used by permission.

[46]Hyles, p. 122.

[47]Angel Martinez, *The Fountain of Youth* (Grand Rapids: Zondervan Publishing House, 1957), p. 23.

[48]Kent, p. 18.

[49]Hyles, p. 125.

[50]Bedsole, p. 128.

[51]Hyles, p. 127.

CHAPTER III

THE PHILOSOPHY OF CHURCH GROWTH

The man who goes to a city where he is unknown, to build a church that as yet has no members, no facilities, no property, and no organization or name, must have the right philosophy of church growth if he establishes a church in that city. The man who moves to an established church to pastor must also have the right philosophy if his church is to grow. By philosophy is meant the basic principles upon which churches are built.

Wrong Philosophies of Church Growth

Not all churches want to grow. Small churches with entrenched lay leaders who fear they will lose their positions of power if they win the dynamic leaders in their community do not want to grow. If a church wants to grow, the leaders must be prepared to move over and make room for new leadership as the Lord provides.

The church that is so infected with negative piety that members are afraid someone will come into their ranks who is not saved or who does not share their standards or beliefs does not want to grow. The growing church will get people saved and teach them its doctrines and standards.

The church that believes it is big enough or that it is God's will for it to be small does not want to grow. A church must never stop growing. When a church stops growing it begins to die.

The church that fears the construction of buildings, debts,

added staff, and financial campaigns involved if it grows does not want to grow.[1]

Churches of the past have made wrong basic assumptions that have kept them small. Some have believed that the small church is more effective than the large church. A small church is not wrong. But a church that wants to stay small is wrong because it says, "I want to get few people saved, I want to minister to few people, I want to help few people, I only want a few people." The small church does not want to minister to its city, because many people might come and join it, and the church would no longer be small. The large church can offer an effective total church program that the small church cannot.

Another wrong assumption of the past has been that the church should be in the community. The idea was to have a housing development with the church in the middle of it. This thinking has resulted in untold thousands of churches off the beaten path, in hard to get to, out of the way places. Examples are numerous where a Baptist church is on one corner of the block, across the street is the Methodist church, across the other way is the Presbyterian church, and diagonally across is the Pentecostal church, and all of them combined do not have enough attending to make a good congregation. It is wrong to assume that a small portion of a community can support a church. The church needs to draw from the entire city and it needs to locate so it can.

Churches of the past have believed that parking is unimportant. That is why many downtown churches have buildings costing hundreds of thousands of dollars and no off the street parking at all. People will not drive several miles to a church if there is no place to park when they arrive. If a church is to grow it must have surplus parking.

The pastor will do well to realize that certain things will keep a church from growing. The idea that church growth just happens without any real reason or effort by the church or its leadership will restrict growth. Most churches that fail do so simply because they never really planned to succeed. A church needs to look at its city and see how it could reach that city for Christ. If the church would sense its responsibility for the people of its city and draw plans to reach those people, that church would grow by leaps and bounds.[2]

A boring program keeps many churches from growing. They will not allow any music that will stir the hearts of people. The preacher has no fire or enthusiasm in his preaching, and the entire service is a series of "uprisings and down sittings" because the pastor and people "do not want to lower the dignity of the gospel."

The Sunday morning service should be the most lively, interesting, appealing, evangelistic service possible because more unsaved people go to church on Sunday morning than any other time. There is absolutely no excuse for the bearers of the glorious gospel of Christ to be anything but enthusiastic, exciting, and dynamic.

The pastor who emphasizes fear, hate, and anger instead of faith, hope, love, and joy will preach to small crowds. People will not rush in to overflow churches that generate fear and anger.

Instant success can cause a church to relax and lose its burden and stop growing. No church can continue growing if it depends on members from other churches and people of its denomination moving to town for church growth. Unless a church gets out and reaches the unsaved of its city, it does not deserve to grow.[3]

Fear of increasing indebtedness has kept many churches from growing. Rather than borrow money for more space and additional parking, they have declined in number and finance. If a church needs to take a step of faith and refuses to do so, it will always decline.

The church not convinced of its ministry and message will not grow. If the pastor is not convinced the church is needed, or he is not convinced that its doctrines and ministries are better than any other church's, he should not go there. Churches that refuse to put their full name on their signs, or are afraid for people to find out what they believe, will only convince people that they should not go to that church.

Shortsighted leadership is one principal hindrance to church growth. Because of the result of short-term pastorates many churches have no long-range plans. When a man moves to a city to begin or pastor a church, he should plan to spend his life there and make his church growth plans accordingly.[4]

Impossibility thinking keeps many churches from growing. Impossibility thinkers are people who react to any positive suggestions with a number of reasons why "it can't be done." They are people with no faith who produce doubt, stimulate fear, and generate a mental climate of pessimism which causes the people of God to wander in the wilderness when they could have possessed the promised land.[5]

Distractions have diverted the attention and energy from their evangelistic mission in many churches. Activities have distracted many from the primary objective of winning souls. Many leaders, both laymen and ministers, get preoccupied with programs or causes which have little to do with the propagation of the gospel and nothing to do with finding the lost.[6]

Right Philosophies of Church Growth

Churches can grow today. There are opportunities everywhere. America is more "winnable" today than in the days of
George Washington or the Gold Rush because of the availablity
of the Bible, the dedicated Christians in the land, the tools and
methods to do the job, and the abundance of funds. The church
needs to analyze its situation, study growth methods, determine
the right course of action, and reach all she can for Christ.[7]

There are some basic laws that determine whether a church
grows or not. First, *the pastor and people believe in and
magnify the Bible as the infallible Word of God.* The Bible is the
textbook of the church to be preached, believed, studied, and
followed. It is the rule book for all the church says and does.

*There is a deep personal commitment to the Lordship of
Christ and to obeying the Great Commission.* Rather than
conforming to the ways of the world, the church seeks to win
people to Christ and change their lives to conform to the
teachings of the Bible. This results in high standards, clean
living, faithful attendance, earnest prayer, and constant witnessing on the part of the membership.

*Evangelism or soul-winning is the number one priority of
the church.* Every organization in the church is expected to
engage in evangelism. The time, energy, and money devoted to
any activity or organization is in direct proportion to its
evangelism productivity. A good amount from the church
budget is designated specifically for evangelism. Nothing is
permitted to take the place of the evangelistic emphasis or
services in the church. The church's main business is reaching
the lost and it should be given top priority.

Another basic law of church growth is that *the pastor is*

the leader of the church. He is Christ's undershepherd whom He has sent to lead the church in its task of fulfilling the Great Commission. He is filled, controlled, and guided by the Holy Spirit. He is a man of clear vision, great faith, and a burden for a lost world. His personal vision and dedication lead the church in a program of world evangelization with a special emphasis upon their Jerusalem. The success of the church rests heavily upon the vision, burden, and leadership of the pastor. Leadership is not dictatorship. As the shepherd, he does not get behind and drive the sheep. Neither does he slaughter the sheep, but he leads them and feeds them. The pastor will do well to follow the example of the Good Shepherd of John 10:11 who " . . . giveth his life for the sheep," because of His love for them. People will follow a pastor anywhere if they know he loves them. The church will love if the pastor loves. The people will go if the pastor goes. The members will work if the pastor works. The church will succeed if the pastor succeeds. Church building is a matter of leadership. Unless the pastor recognizes and assumes that leadership, all efforts at building will fail.[8]

The Good Shepherd said that, " . . . when he putteth forth his own sheep, he goeth before them, and the sheep follow him: for they know his voice" (John 10:4). The leader does not get so far ahead of the flock that he runs off and leaves them. Although he stays in front, he takes them with him. He stays within talking range at all times. He does not obligate the church financially himself, but he includes the sheep in the plans. He is out in front, but they all go into it together. Then, when the payments are due, the sheep are there to help pay. When the pastor takes his rightful place as the leader of the church, the people are the most informed and included of any people.

If a church has the right philosophy of church growth *both the pastor and the church have a vision of reaching their entire city for Christ and prepare the church for an influx of people.* They will draw no boundary lines and have no class systems, but practice saturation evangelism, which means to get the gospel to every available person with every available means at every available time.[9] The local church is the instrument of Christ to bring the gospel to everyone in the world, and should be the launching pad for evangelistic ministry, soul-winning, enlistment, and Christian training.[10] This means that the church should use every means available to reach everyone possible.

The church with the right philosophy will *use the church growth methods that God is blessing.* The first of these should be soul-winning. God has always blessed the sharing of the gospel on a one-to-one basis. Today is no exception. Soul-winning is the least expensive and most rewarding method the church can use. Soul-winning simply means, "witnessing the gospel to the total personality of man in his sinful condition so that he may respond to Christ in evangelism."[11] Witnessing is sharing the personal testimony. The total personality involves the intellect, emotions, and will. Each person must realize his sinful condition before God. His response to Christ is belief and repentance. Personal evangelism is the dynamic influence behind pulpit evangelism. God will bless the church with growth where the pastor and members are engaged in evangelism.[12] The man who builds a strong church today must have the right philosophy on soul-winning himself and organize and train his people to be soul-winners.

The bus ministry is a method which is being used effectively in many growing churches.[13] The bus ministry is an evangelistic arm of the church that reaches into its neighborhoods and brings adults and children to church.[14] The bus ministry is being blessed of God because it is getting churches involved in the New Testament way of reaching people, which is house-to-house, door-to-door witnessing. Most of the growing churches today have bus ministries. The pastor who wants a growing church will be, wise to invest his time and money in those things that are reaching people. The bus ministry is certainly one of these. Many believe the bus ministry to be the most powerful productive means available to local churches to reach the masses.[15]

Extensive advertisement is another characteristic of churches that are growing. Many means of advertisement are available to the church today such as newspaper, radio, television, telephone, signs, billboards, handbills, brochures, and bulk mailings. The best advertisement is that of personal witnessing of the members. Advertisement is making known to the people what the church has to offer, where it is, and when people are to come. Many churches feel so strongly about the importance of advertisment that they allocate a large part of the church budget for this purpose.

Promotion is another effective method which must be used in church growth. To promote something means to advance it by stirring up interest in it. Because of the use of unscriptural or distasteful promotional ideas, some have labeled all promotion as bad and forbidden its use in the church. But if a promotional technique is Scriptural and fits in with the Biblical aims of the church, it is right to use. Promotions are used to "win a hearing" to get the unsaved under the sound of the gospel. If God blesses those techniques and souls are saved, and others are not repelled from the church, it cannot be wrong. It is wrong, rather, not to promote and let one's city go to Hell when some ingenuity could be used to get people to Christ. Promotions such as special speakers, special singers, special guests, enlargement campaigns, contests, high attendance days, and gifts to various people are some promotional ideas that can be used.[16] More will be said about advertisement and promotion later, but before a man moves to a city to build a church, he needs the right philosophy of promotion for church growth.

Another philosophy of growing churches is that *worship services are geared to reach the lost.* Services must be evangelistic. Formal services hinder soul-winning. Formalism is the opposite of Biblical Christianity and has always marked the departure from soul-winning.[17] Formalism turns the Sunday morning service into a time when people follow a printed schedule from which they dare not deviate, the preacher prays a formal prayer that is sometimes read, the choir chants a response, the music is composed of anthems, the sermon is quiet, cold, and dignified, and the invitation is just a ritual. If a church is to win souls it must renounce this false concept of a worship service and turn to the informality of the New Testament and make every service evangelistic, especially the Sunday morning service.[18]

Goal setting is a very important church growth principle. Success or failure starts at this point, for goal setting is nothing more than planning ahead. When one fails to plan, he plans to fail. When no goals are set for growth, goals are set for no growth. Failure to set successful goals assures failure.[19]

Some churches and pastors are opposed to goal setting for various reasons. Some are opposed to setting goals because they do not stay in one place very long. When goals are set, the preacher obligates himself to stay and reach them. Others oppose setting goals for fear of failure. However, it is better to try something and only accomplish part of it than to attempt nothing and accomplish it all. Only dreams that are publicly announced become goals. It is better for a church to attempt something great and fail than to attempt to do nothing and succeed.[20]

Of course, wisdom should be used to set realistic goals that are high enough to challenge the faith of the church but low enough that they are realistic. Some ways to determine if goals are attainable are:

(1) Will it excite the people and motivate them to want to reach it?

(2) Is it something that is worthwhile in helping people?

(3) Is it so common place that it is unimaginative?

(4) Is your church the first in the area to try it?[21]

Some goals that could be set are: attendance, membership, baptisms, finances, missions, and program goals. These goals should not simply be drawn out of the air, but arrived at by careful planning and prayer by the pastor and leaders of the church.[22]

A total church program geared to minister to all people is another philosophy essential to a growing church. The services are planned to reach as many people as possible. Once people are brought to church, the service is conducted so as to get them down the aisle for public profession of salvation. Then counselors are prepared to deal with those who respond. An extensive follow-up program is begun to conserve the results and train those won and involve them in the outreach of the church. Laymen are trained and challenged in soul-winning. Everything done for any age is done in the best possible fashion to make the church the best it can be and appealing to all.

In growing churches, *the pastor and church maintain high standards of Christian living and practice separation from the world.* Standards and convictions must be instilled in the lives of church members and must be Bible based. Growing churches are separated churches. If the church does not challenge people to clean up their lives and dedicate themselves to faithful service for Christ, it will be difficult for that church to get the kind of dedication and service from its members that is necessary to build a church.

The main dependence in a growing church is not on men or methods, but on prayer, the Word of God, and the power of the Holy Spirit. It was Christ who said, " . . . upon this rock I will build my church; and the gates of hell shall not prevail against it" (Matt. 16:18). The Old Testament said, "Except the Lord build the house, they labor in vain that build it . . . " (Psalm 127:1).

The pastor or church planter with the right philosophy who goes to a city determined to declare all the counsel of God, spends much time in prayer, plans his work and works his plan, can succeed in building a strong, Bible-believing, soul-winning church.

Conclusion

A man's philosophy of church growth will largely determine the success of his ministry. Unless he intends to do what is necessary to build a church, he should not get involved. The church's philosophy will be his philosophy.

He must plan prayerfully, carefully, and then lovingly lead the church into those programs which will result in growth. The church that wants to grow can grow. If a pastor will lead his church into growth methods, his people will follow him and the Lord will bless him for it. He will be victorious in his ministry rather than defeated.

Chapter III
Reference Notes

[1]Robert Schuller, *Your Church Has Real Possibilities* (Glendale, California: Regal Books, 1974), pp. 34-36. Used by permission.

[2]Donald McGavran and Win Arn, *How to Grow a Church* (Glendale, California: Regal Books, 1973), p. 171. Used by permission.

[3]Schuller, pp. 10-14.

[4]*Ibid.*, pp. 34-40.

[5]*Ibid.*, pp. 44-45.

[6]McGavran and Arn, p. 42.

[7]*Ibid.*, p. 56.

[8]Charles M. Underwood, editor, *Planting the Independent Fundamental Church* (Greenville, South Carolina: Bob Jones University, 1972), p. 60.

[9]Jerry Falwell and Elmer Towns, *Church Aflame* (Nashville: Impact Books, 1971), p. 70.

[10]*Ibid.*

[11]*Ibid.*, p. 56.

[12]*Ibid.*

[13]Lee Lebsack, *Ten at the Top* (Stow, Ohio: New Hope Press, 1974), p. 7.

[14]Falwell and Towns, p. 112.

[15]*Ibid.*, p. 79.

[16]*Ibid.*, p. 88.

[17]John R. Rice, *Why Our Churches Do Not Win Souls* (Murfreesboro, Tennessee: Sword of the Lord, 1966), p. 86.

[18]*Ibid.*, p. 87.

[19]Schuller, p. 72.

[20]*Ibid.*, p. 75.

[21]*Ibid.*, p. 76.

[22]*Ibid.*, p. 77.

CHAPTER IV

LAYING A FOUNDATION

One of the very important requirements in starting a new church is preplanning. Experience has shown that the man who does this foundational work six months to a year before he starts conducting services will build a better and stronger local church.[1]

The Matter of Sponsorship

After the church planter has settled on the city to which God wants him to go, he must settle the question of sponsorship. Shall he move to the city and get himself a secular job to support his family and start the church by "making tents"? Many churches have been successfully started in this way. Or, shall he go under the sponsorship of the National Home Missions Board? The latter appears to be the most successful method for a number of reasons. First, it is a Scriptural method. As Paul and Barnabas went out to establish churches, they were sent by the Antioch Church (Acts 13:2, 3). This meant that they were not only sent by the Holy Ghost, but the church as well. This makes the endeavor of starting the new church an effort of the whole group of sponsoring churches and not just the preacher alone. It can mean much to the church planter and his family to know that they are not alone in starting this new church, but their entire denomination stands with them in prayer and financial support.

To go under the sponsorship of a board is the way

churches of many denominations are begun.[2] Others advise church planters to contact relatives, friends, and independent churches by either visits or letters explaining the amount needed for salary to start the new church and solicit their help.[3]

The new church so supported has a greater opportunity for success because the church planter can devote his full time to this new work.[4] When a church planter goes out as a national home missionary, his application is reviewed, his references contacted, and he is personally interviewed by the National Home Missions Board. This is a tremendous boost to a man's self-confidence that this is God's will for him to establish a church in this particular city. The period of waiting involved while his application is being processed helps the preacher and his family to pray and settle the matter more completely about the will of God for them. Once the preacher is approved, he is put on the prayer list of all the Bible colleges. His name appears in the publications of the Woman's National Auxiliary Convention, which brings the prayer support of thousands of women. His picture is published in *Mission Grams*, which has a name mailing list. These things result in thousands of people standing with the missionary in prayer support. The church planter would not have this kind of prayer support if he went on his own.

By going under the sponsorship of the National Home Missions Board he will have the opportunity to visit churches to raise prayer and financial support. This usually not only results in needed support being raised, but also in a number of names and addresses of prospects who have moved to the city where he plans to start the church. Some of these may prove to be the nucleus around which the new church will be built.[5] In many cases, God will speak to the hearts of dedicated laymen during these itinerant services which will result in these couples moving to the city with the missionary to help start the church.

By going under the National Home Missions Board the missionary is paid a liveable salary and is able to put his full time into the work of starting the church. This enables the church to grow much faster and become self-supporting much sooner. Such a church, begun by a full-time pastor, will always be convinced of the need of a pastor who is fully supported so that he can put his full time into the ministry.

Once the matter has been settled of where and how the church planter will raise needed support, he will want to make preparations to get to the field.

Before Arrival in the City

There are a number of things the church planter can do before he moves to the city that will help him get the church started more easily. He should write the Chamber of Commerce in the city and obtain all the information he can from them. This organization knows many details of the area and will gladly supply materials that will be invaluable.[6] A church directory should be requested from them. This will let the church planter know the number and kinds of churches in the city.[7] The growth rate of the city is important also. The Chamber of Commerce will know how many new families are moving to the city each month. They are also a good source to find the newcomer lists for the city. They will send the information on the industries and businesses of the city, the average income, cost of housing, living costs as compared to other sections of the country, and growth patterns. They will furnish information

about schools, colleges, amusements, places of interest, hospitals, radio and television stations, and newspapers.[8]

Another important item to be acquired as soon as possible
is a good city map. The Chamber of Commerce or a stationery
shop in the city will have one. Once this map is acquired it
should be studied carefully before the preacher's relocation to
the new city. The church planter can learn the interstates and
main arteries of the city. He can memorize the main streets. He
can locate the hospitals, industries, points of interest, and other
places of importance so that he will be acquainted with the city
even before he moves there. This alone will save him many
hours that he would have spent looking for places.[9]

A telephone directory of the city is another important
item to obtain before moving to the city. In one's contact with
the Chamber of Commerce he should check with them about
how to obtain a commercial telephone directory arranged by
streets rather than alphabetically. In almost all large cities such
a telephone book can be obtained. It will give the church
planter information about the size of families, number of
houses, home values, and income levels in various sections of
the city. These two city telephone directories can be studied
along with the city map and help to familiarize the missionary
with the city.[10]

Before moving to the city, the preacher should gather the
equipment he will need. He will need a good typewriter. His
letters and printed materials will not look neat unless he has a
good typewriter. If he can possibly afford an IBM Selectric
electric typewriter, the missionary would do well to obtain
one.

He will also need a good mimeograph machine of some kind
that is in good working condition. He should have a desk, book-

case, and file cabinet for his office.

He should have a dependable car. It does not have to be new or expensive, but one that will start, especially in cold areas, and one that runs well. It is always a problem for a preacher, but he needs to keep his payments as low as possible. If he could get as many needed equipment items paid for as possible before he goes to the city, it will greatly help.

Another consideration in the way of equipment is a good church bus. A preacher could purchase a bus, stack the seats in the front part, place his furniture in the back, attach his car to the rear bumper with a tow bar, and move to the city in that manner. Moving expense would go a long way toward the purchase of the bus. He could paint the name of the church on the side. It would not only advertise his church, but serve as the beginning of his bus fleet for the new church.[11]

Once the preacher has completed his work at the church he is leaving, he should set up a special bank account for the new church, preferably at a bank in the city where he will later move, and begin to pay his tithes to the new church during the months of preparation. This will give the church planter a good amount of money to use for renting a meeting place, advertising, purchase of equipment, and the many things he will need to start services in the new church.

The missionary should work on sermons and get as many prepared as possible before he moves to the city so that he can spend more time visiting in the beginning months of the new church.[12]

He can also write his church constitution and bylaws during the months he is preparing to move to the city. More will be said later about this document, but it needs some real time, thought, and prayer spent on it to make sure the new church is organized to function properly.

The church planter, during his itineration work to raise support, should be on the lookout for equipment and supplies he can use. If he goes as a national home missionary, he will receive free of charge fifty new *Free Will Baptist Hymn Books* and Sunday school literature, but he will need offering plates, clerk's books, treasurer's books, offering envelopes, visitors' cards, tracts, and many other items. These could all be gathered and stored for moving to the new city.[13]

If possible, the missionary should visit the city before moving. He could secure a realtor and find a home. This would allow time for the loan to be processed so that when he does move to the city, he could move directly to his own home. He would avoid moving twice. While there to purchase a home he could visit the Chamber of Commerce and gather some additional information. He could visit the city planning commission and learn about proposed housing developments. He could open a bank account and get acquainted with the banker. He might subscribe to the newspapers so that he could keep abreast of events in the new city. This visit will help the pastor become better acquainted with the city, and it will give God the opportunity to burden his soul with the vision of its lost multitudes.

It is best for the missionary to buy his own house rather than renting. Owning his own home will convey to his city a sense of permanence and let the residents know he intends to stay. It will give him the privileges of a property owner in the city and give his family a sense of security. Owning a home will also keep the preacher from packing and leaving in a time of discouragement. It will also yield a substantial savings for the pastor and his family in the years he is struggling and sacrificing to start the new church.[14]

The time spent in preparation will pay large dividends when the preacher moves to the city with his support raised, supplies gathered, materials prepared, and his home purchased so that he can concentrate on reaching people and training them to serve in the new church.

After Arrival in the City

The pastor and his family must begin immediately to unload and unpack their belongings. He must get utilities turned on and the telephone installed. His name should be listed with the title of "Pastor" or "Reverend" in the telephone directory so people will know he is a preacher. As soon as he gets the telephone number he should find a printer and place an order for the brochures and supplies he will need when he begins his visitation. Then he should return to the unpacking and stay with it until everything is unpacked and in place. He should not begin his church work until all this is completed. His family will need the security of a well-ordered household in this new city where they are strangers. Once the work begins, there will be no time for unpacking, and it is not good for people to visit the home and see boxes sitting everywhere. People will wonder if the preacher plans to stay in town.[15]

When the preacher gets his family moved in and the children enrolled in school if necessary, he should get his new driver's license and license plates for his car. Even though the state may not require new license that soon, it will be poor advertisement for the preacher to visit homes if he has out of state license plates on his car. As soon as possible the pastor and his family should establish permanent residence in every way possible. They should not refer to the way it was "back home," but make this city their home as soon as possible. People will respond much better to those who love their city.

Once the family is moved in and settled, the preacher is ready to begin his work. He should write some well-worded, double-spaced, news releases and take them, with a black and white glossy picture of himself, to every newspaper within a thirty-mile radius of the city. He will want to meet the editors personally and give them the pictures and news releases along with his plans for beginning the new church. Many of them will publish the story free of charge, and the preacher will establish a relationship with the news media.

Next he should visit the radio and television stations and meet the managers. These contacts may also open the way for some free advertisement for the new church.[16]

In his travels about the city in those first days, the church planter should always keep his eyes open for a meeting place for the services. It is not essential at this point that the meeting place be secured, because it should be at least a month before services are actually started; but facilities will be needed, so it will pay to be watching.

Any families who are prospects and might be interested in helping the new church get started should be visited and a cordial relationship established as soon as possible.

There is always a strong temptation to begin services the first Sunday the new preacher is in town, but it is not best to begin services until extensive groundwork has been laid. It is very important that the first Sunday's attendance be as large as possible. It will give the pastor, his family, and those who attend the sense of assurance that the Lord is leading in the new church.[17]

The first several days will be taken up with these preliminary activities of unpacking, getting car license, meeting the news media, and visiting any families who might be prospects. By this time the brochures should be ready from the printers. So bright and early on Monday morning the preacher should begin his visitation to invite people to a "get acquainted meeting" in his home or another appropriate meeting place, which will be on Tuesday night of the following week. He should visit in a different section of town each day and spend all the time possible for an entire month in visitation. He should start about nine o'clock Monday morning and visit all day, spending eight to ten hours in visitation. In these visits he should not go in, but simply meet people at the door, tell them who he is, explain about the beginning of the new church, and invite them to a "get acquainted meeting" on Tuesday night of the following week. He should give them one of the brochures and move on to the next house. If he works hard, he should be able to visit 150 homes or more in a single day.

The next day he should go to a different section of the city. Visiting different areas of the city will give the pioneer pastor a greater burden for the city. It will also show people that the new church is to be a metropolitan church rather than a community church. It will also keep the nucleus of the church from being composed of just one group of people. Cities are usually built in sections. Older people will live in one section, Catholics will live predominantly in one section, and Baptists or other Protestants might live in another. People often move to different sections of town because of likenesses. Some sections are liberal while others are conservative. Politicians know this and know the sections where they can get the most votes.

The preacher should visit every day, a minimum of forty

hours a week, and more if possible. During these weeks of
visitation he might want to visit ten or twelve hours a day for
four days and then take one day to work on his printing,
advertising, and getting things ready for the first services.

This door-to-door visitation should not be for the purpose
of soul-winning or doctrinal teaching, but simply to invite those
interested to the Tuesday night "get acquainted meeting." Of
course, there will be some who will want to talk, and the
preacher must write down names and addresses of prospects for
his mailing list and those who need return calls, but primarily he
goes down the street knocking on every door inviting the people
to the Tuesday night meeting. The address of the meeting place
will be on the brochures which he gives out. He will also want
to call on all prospects he is acquainted with to get them out to
the meeting.

At the first Tuesday night "get acquainted meeting" the
pastor should begin by introducing himself and his family,
telling the people some things about himself such as where he is
from and what he has done in the Lord's work. Then he should
give the people, one after the other, a chance to introduce
themselves to each other. After everyone knows each person
present, he should introduce the people to the new church. He
should explain how God burdened his heart for the city and
how he has come to preach the gospel to the people so they can
be saved, can know they are saved, and can be assured that they
will go to Heaven when they die.

Then the preacher should move right into the plan of
salvation, explaining carefully exactly how a person is saved. He
has now introduced the people to himself, his family, his
church, and his Savior. Then he should ask for heads to be
bowed for dismissal. While heads are bowed he should ask for a

show of hands of any who are not sure of their relationship to God. The pastor may let the Lord lead him at this time as to how to further pursue the invitation. He might want to proceed with refreshments and invite any who are interested to remain after the others are gone. Dismiss the meeting with an invitation to the   second Tuesday night meeting when he will be introducing the people to another part of the new church.

The next morning the preacher should begin visiting for the second Tuesday night meeting. With another solid week of visitation and calling all the prospects, the second Tuesday night meeting should have a larger attendance. The new group will need to be introduced to those who have returned from the first Tuesday night meeting. Then explain to them the doctrines of the church. Explain to them what the church believes about Heaven, Hell, the inspiration of the Scriptures, the fall of man, the person and work of Christ, salvation through repentance and faith, baptism, and the church. This should not be a long discourse, but just a brief statement on each doctrine with a verse of Scripture to support it.

At the close of that meeting, a six months' financial budget of the church should be distributed which has been previously prepared. It will need to be a simple budget with rent on the building, supplies, ten percent going to worldwide evangelism, advertising, and the pastor's salary. Although the pastor is receiving his support as a missionary or from friends and supporters, the new church should begin immediately to start assuming his salary and make the church self-supporting as soon as possible.

When the budget is distributed and explained, a few words will need to be said about tithing, asking the people to take the budget home with them to pray about their financial support for the new church.

The next morning begins another week with a minimum of forty hours of visitation toward the third Tuesday night meeting. In this meeting the pastor will need to tell the people about the kind of church he plans to have, what he hopes the church will do, and the philosophies to make the church grow. He will want to explain the youth program, the soul-winning and outreach ministries, and the goals he has in mind for the church. The meeting will be closed by distributing a copy of the budget to the new people attending and explaining to the people about the first worship service which will be the following Sunday. By this time excitement should be mounting as three hard weeks of visitation and three Tuesday night "get acquainted meetings" have been conducted to prepare for the first Sunday's services.[18]

The First Sunday

The church planter should lay plans carefully for this first Sunday's services. By this time he will have chosen the meeting place, whether it be a vacant church, a school, a fire hall, a community hall, a union hall, an empty factory, a veteran's hall, a warehouse, or an empty store front building.[19] The pastor could ask God to provide the building rent free. This has been the case in many pioneer works. However, if rent must be paid, the new church must be as conservative as possible and stay within the budget item allocated for rent.

After securing the building, the pastor must make whatever immediate improvements are needed. He should make the building as attractive as possible by cleaning, painting, repairing, and remodeling if necessary. The necessary arrangements should be made to make sure everything is ready by way of equipment and supplies for the first Sunday. A nice sign will need to be prepared marking the place so the people can find it easily. This sign should be attractively lettered displaying the church's name, the meeting schedule, the pastor's name and telephone number. The pastor should check with local officials about building codes so as not to violate any ordinances.

A large ad should be put in the newspapers advertising the grand opening of the new church. If possible, it should be a half page ad in the most widely circulated newspaper in the city.[20] This needs to be carefully prepared, as it will be the first impression of the church that most people will receive. The ad should not appear more than one week ahead of the first Sunday's service. Sometimes such an ad can also be put in a circular or shopper-type paper that is delivered to every house. This ad will cost several hundred dollars, but if done properly, will acquaint a large segment of the city with the new church. A half page ad is recommended because everyone who looks through the paper will see it.[21]

Sometimes the smaller area papers will put news items in free of charge. Some spot announcements on the radio and television announcing the grand opening should be secured if possible. It will cost to advertise properly for this first Sunday, but it will be money well spent.

This advertisement should include a picture of the pastor, some information about the church, and the date and place of the first service in large letters. This will get the preacher's name and face before the city.

After the advertisement has been taken care of, arrangements must be made to see that everything is ready for the first service. First, the meeting place will need to look as nice as possible and made to look as much like a church as possible. A pulpit and an altar must be secured. Offering plates need to be on hand and hymnbooks arranged so the people can easily obtain them. A treasurer will need to be appointed and a treasurer's book purchased. Offering envelopes, visitor's cards, new convert packets, and follow-up materials need to be on hand. A display should be prepared with literature about the church and denomination. Make sure there is a well-tuned piano, and all furniture clean and dusted.

From the people gathered in the Tuesday night "get acquainted meetings" choose some ushers and explain to them how to obtain visitor's cards, how to receive the offering, and how to keep the building properly ventilated. Have some greeters to meet the people as they come in the door. Have some ladies to take babies to the nursery, and make sure there are two responsible ladies as nursery attendants on this special occasion. Someone will need to stay at the door to assist those who come in late.

The music is very important on that first Sunday. If possible, a good soloist, trio, or quartet should be secured. With proper planning perhaps people from the preacher's home church could be present on that first Sunday to provide special music. Arrangements need to be made for a good pianist and song leader. The songs should be selected ahead of time, and the entire order of service carefully planned. If bulletins are used, these should be printed clearly, perhaps even by a professional printer for this first service.

Several personalities should be invited to this special first service. The mayor, the city councilmen, a state representative, the banker, the chief of police, and many other public figures should be contacted, with an explanation as to what will happen and their presence requested. If they consent to come and bring words of welcome to the new church, this could be included in the advertisement. This could result in other city officials and reporters attending, which will add to the crowd and publicity of the new church.

Some special groups could be invited such as senior citizens, scout troops, firemen, policemen, and various clubs and organizations. Out of town friends should be invited, with the pastor and his family doing everything possible to get a good crowd present on the first Sunday.

This special first Sunday is so very important. There will be people present who are curiosity seekers. The pastor should prepare a good sermon with care, one that will present Christ and stir hearts without antagonizing people. Some people should be trained as altar workers to deal with those who respond to the invitation.

Extreme care should be taken to get visitor's cards from all the people. Copies of the budget should be distributed to all who have not as yet received copies.

This first Sunday should be a Sunday morning preaching service only. It is best not to try to have Sunday school on the first Sunday. Begin with a Sunday morning and Sunday evening preaching service that first Sunday, and start the Sunday school on the second Sunday.

If the pastor has visited and advertised properly, and bathed the occasion in prayer, the new church should begin with a glorious first Sunday. Some people may be saved and the whole group will go away with the assurance that the new church will succeed.

Conclusion

The foundation of any building is always the most tedious part of the building and the part that is the least visible. But it is the part upon which the whole building rests.

The suggestions set forth in this chapter may seem small and unnecessary. The church planter may grow impatient to begin services without the detailed preparation outlined here. However, if he will do the things suggested and follow the plan as outlined, he will get his church off to a good start and gather about him a group of enthusiastic people, thus eliminating much of the struggle in starting the new church.

Chapter IV
Reference Notes

[1]Grant C. Rice, *Principles of New Church Planting* (Rockvale, Tennessee: Grant C. Rice Church Planting—Consulting, 1977), p. 1.

[2]Robert Schuller, *Your Church Has Real Possibilities* (Glendale, California: Regal Books, 1974), foreword. Used by permission.

[3]Rice, p. 1.

[4]Tom Lilly, *Building a New Church* (Nashville: Free Will Baptist Home Missions Board, 1971), p. 2.

[5]Elmer Towns, *Getting a Church Started in the Face of Insurmountable Odds with Limited Rooources in Unlikely Circumstances* (Nashville: Impact Books, 1975), p. 151.

[6]Rice, p. 2.

[7]*Ibid.*

[8]Max Helton, "How to Get Set Up," (Hammond, Indiana: Helton Publications, n.d.).

[9]*Ibid.*

[10]*Ibid.*

[11]*Ibid.*

[12]Rice, p. 3.

[13]Roy Thomas, *How to Start a Church from Scratch* (Nashville: Free Will Baptist Home Missions Board, 1971), p. 2.

[14]*Ibid.*, p. 3.

[15]Helton, "How to Get Set Up."

[16]*Ibid.*

[17]Thomas, p. 3.

[18]Helton, "How to Get Set Up."

[19]Thomas, p. 3.

[20]Lyle Wacker, *Church Extension Handbook* (Forest Park, Illinois: North American Baptist Missionary Society, n.d.), p. 4.

[21]Helton, "The First Sunday," (Hammond, Indiana: Helton Publications, n.d.).

CHAPTER V

THE ORGANIZATIONAL STRUCTURE

Once the first service is held, the church planter must not feel that the work is done. It is just beginning. He must organize this group into a Bible-believing, Bible-teaching, Bible-practicing, soul-winning church.

After the First Sunday

Beginning on Monday, he should send a letter to everyone who attended the first Sunday. His wife possibly could help with typing and secretarial work until a church secretary can be hired. He should call on every family who came, expressing his gratitude for their presence.

On the second Sunday, the Sunday school should be started. The pastor should teach the adult class, his wife a teenage class, and secure some other qualified person for a children's class. Someone could be placed in the nursery or cradle roll. The pastor should start with only a few classes and add others as qualified teachers become available. Unqualified teachers are worse than no teachers at all. So Sunday school standards need to be established at the very beginning so that the Sunday school will get off to a good start.

The next thing the pastor should begin is a teacher training class. The Evangelical Teacher Training Association (ETTA) courses are very good for this purpose. The Sunday School and Church Training Department also has a very fine course of books, all written by our people, which can be used.

The pastor will also want to begin a follow-up program for those won to Christ. It should begin in the home at the outset. Appointments can be made to come to the converts' homes during the week to review and discuss the National Home Missions Department's *Follow-Up Lessons for New Converts to Christ* until all thirteen lessons are completed.

Arrangements should be made to baptize those who need it as soon as possible. Many church planters neglect this important area, but people will grow spiritually when they are baptized. It will take some effort to rent a church for this purpose, but the matter should not be delayed.

The Constitution and Bylaws

The church planter should have begun work on this important document months before moving to the city. It needs to be studied prayerfully. The constitution and bylaws are important to see that the church is started right and continues right until the Lord returns.[1] The constitution of the church is primarily a document of principles   which is   the foundation upon which the church life and operation are structured, and which will not change except by vote of the church. The bylaws are to implement the principles enunciated in the constitution. Therefore they must be flexible reflecting the changes occurring in the church from its growth and increased outreach.[2]

The constitution will set forth the name of the church and its purpose for existence.[3] This will be important for legal matters in the future. The church affiliation will show that the church is affiliated with the National Association of Free Will Baptists. This will help keep others from stealing the church and will set forth the doctrines as those described in *A Treatise of the Faith and Practices of the Original Free Will Baptists.*[4]

The membership of the church should be defined, and how members are received will need to be stated. There should be sections dealing with ministers and their families who join the church, and a section on an inactive list, which is an efficient way of handling the unfortunate situation of inactive members. The discipline of the membership is explained, giving both the method and the spirit with which it should be done.

In the section dealing with church officers, their qualifications should be clearly stated. Here the pastor will require church membership and faithful active support of all the church ministries. In the article describing the pastor, a pastor-led church should be organized with the pastor on an indefinite call rather than an annual call. The qualifications and duties of deacons are described.

Some are of the opinion that the church should have no committees.[5] Some believe that no church can be effectively run by a series of committees and that the church should have none.[6] However, if the pastor chooses the committee members and supervises their work, the committees are not controlling the church. Rather, the pastor has just had some foresight into future work that needs to be done and made provision for it in the church constitution. An auditing committee is needed to audit the treasurer's books each year. When the church grows to the place it needs a professional audit, this committee could be dissolved. A Christian education committee is needed to work under the pastor as a planning committee for the educational needs of the church. It is one thing for the pastor to lead the church, but quite another for him to exclude the people from all decisions.

An advisory board should be included which would discuss and pray over business before it is presented to the church. This board acts only as the name suggests, in an advisory capacity.

The meetings the church will have should be put in the constitution. Visitation and soul-winning ministries should be included. The method of finance and denominational support should also be included.

A sample constitution and bylaws follows which the church planter may use as a guide and modify to fit his church's particular needs.

(Suggested Constitution and Bylaws)

Preamble

To the end that all things may be done decently and in order, and that we may more readily help each other in our Christian service, as members of the _____ Church of _____, we adopt the following constitution and bylaws as methods of our work.

Article I

Name and Object

Section 1. Name.

This organization shall be known as the_____

Church of _____

Section 2. Object.

This church, believing in the Bible as the inspired Word of God and the sole rule of faith and practice, and acknowledging its adherence to all the teachings of Christ, is organized for the purpose of the worship of God according to the teachings of His Word, to the practice of the precepts and examples of the church of our Lord Jesus Christ as set forth in the New Testament, to set forth the ordinances and doctrines of the New Testament, and to preach and propagate among all people of the earth the gospel of God's salvation by personal faith in Christ Jesus as Savior and Lord.

Article II

Church Affiliation

Section 1.

This local body of Free Will Baptists shall be a member of the National Association of Free Will Baptists, and shall report regularly by delegation and any necessary letters, and shall become a member of quarterly meetings and associations of the state of _____if/when they are organized.

Article III

Membership

Section 1. Description.

No person shall be accepted as a member of this church in any manner without the will of the church duly expressed by its vote at the next business meeting. He should be acquainted with the doctrines held by the church and subscribe to the constitution and bylaws and *A Treatise of the Faith and Practices of the Original Free Will Baptists.*

Section 2. Admission by experience.

Any person professing faith in the Lord Jesus Christ, giving evidence of salvation, and having studied and accepted the aims and doctrines of the church, may have membership with full privileges except that of voting until the ordinance of baptism has been administered.

Section 3. Admission by letter.

Members from other churches holding like faith may be received by letter with full privileges except that of voting until the letter is received. In the event the letter is not received, it shall be the privilege of the candidate to request full privileges of the church by offering himself for membership on his Christian statement.

Section 4. Admission by statement.

All applicants for membership other than by experience or by
letter, that is, by Christian statement, if previously baptized by
immersion, shall be received into the church in the same way as
those received by experience, except that the ordinance of
baptism shall not be administered. If they have not been
properly baptized, that ordinance shall be required.

Section 5. Dismissal of members.

Any letter of recommendation from this church clerk to the
church he has joined will be granted for any member in full
fellowship and good standing. Any member who wants to leave
the church without joining another church may receive a letter
of dismissal.

Section 6. Ministers and their families.

Ministers and their families are received and dismissed by letter
as other members except when they come from or go to other
denominations,   in which case the advisory board shall be
called to advise respecting the action contemplated.

Section 7. Active members.

The following is an attendance guide for active church
members. They should attend at least seventy-five percent of
the church services and business meetings each year.

Section 8. Inactive members.

When a member shall fail to manifest any interest in the church for a period of three months, showing no desire or intention of returning to the church, such member shall automatically become an inactive member. It shall be the responsibility of the pastor and board of deacons, after due effort to re-establish the member's fellowship with the church, to notify the church clerk of all such lapses of active membership. The clerk having received such instructions shall place the name in question on the inactive list. People whose names are on the inactive list are not to be counted in any official report of the membership and they are not entitled to vote in any business meeting, nor are they entitled to a letter of recommendation. An inactive member may be restored to active membership by the pastor and the board of deacons whenever such a person shall indicate a desire to be reinstated and has given satisfactory assurance of intention to remain faithful to the church.

Section 9. Nonresident active members.

Members who have temporary stays out of town may maintain active membership after they have been absent long enough to be inactive members. But any member who establishes residence in another place shall forfeit his right to vote until his residence is re-established in this area.

Article IV

Discipline

Section 1. Its method and spirit.

Any member having cause of complaint against another must seek to remove it as directed in Matthew 18:15-17. If this is not sufficient, the complaint shall be brought to the attention of the pastor and the board of deacons who shall report their findings and recommend to the church such action as may seem wise and proper. All discipline shall be formulated and carried out in the Spirit of Christ, in meekness and godly fear, lest any fall by the way.

Section 2. Exclusion.

Upon the recommendation of the pastor and the board of deacons and vote of the church, a member guilty of conduct unbecoming of his profession and membership, may be excluded, provided that reason of such contemplated action be given for defense or satisfactory explanation. No member shall be excluded from this church without the privilege of a hearing, if he can be located.

Article V

Organization

Section 1. Officers and standing committees.

The officers of this body shall be pastor, board of deacons, clerk, treasurer, music director, organist, pianist, board of trustees, general Sunday school superintendent, Church Training director, and the following committees: Christian education committee, auditing committee, ushers committee, and other committees which the pastor desires to appoint. There shall also be an advisory board. The term of office for all officers except pastor, deacons, and trustees, shall date from the first Sunday of each church year, and shall be for a term of one year.

Section 2. Qualifications of officers.

All officers shall be members of this church and in good standing as such. They shall work in harmony with the pastor in promoting the aims of the church by faithfully attending the services of the church, visitation, and soul-winning, and by faithfully carrying out the duties of their respective offices. The failure of any officer to fulfill the responsibilities of the office he holds without satisfactory reason shall be considered sufficient reason for the pastor to declare the office vacant.

Section 3. Election of officers.

Officers shall be elected at the _____ (month) business meeting and will take office the first Sunday of the church year. The church year will begin the first Sunday in_____(month).

Article VI

Officers

Section 1. Pastor.

The pastor shall be an ordained minister in good standing with the Free Will Baptist denomination. He shall have charge of and conduct the public services of worship, and the general development of the church shall be under his supervision. He shall be an example to the flock in his dedication, piety, soul-winning, and visitation, and shall do all in his power to promote the interest of the church and to advance the cause of Christ among men. He shall act as moderator of all business meetings of the church. In his absence, the active senior deacon present shall be moderator pro tem. No business meeting, board or committee meeting shall be held of which the pastor is not aware.

The pastor shall be selected and called by the church whenever a vacancy occurs. His election shall take place at a meeting of the church called for that purpose. The purpose of this meeting must be announced at a preceding Sunday service. A two-thirds majority vote of all members present shall be required to elect a pastor. The pastor, thus elected, shall serve at the will of the church subject to termination of service upon sixty days notice on the part of the pastor or church. The deacons may call a special meeting to determine the will of the church at any time by a majority vote of the advisory board. The pastor is an ex officio of all boards and committees.

The pastor shall be paid a salary, the amount to be contingent upon the ability of the church to pay, general living conditions, and the expense involved in maintaining his position. He shall be granted two weeks' paid vacation per year, after he has served the church a year, and three weeks' after he has served the church five years. The church shall pay the pastor's expenses to all denominational meetings of which it is a member.

Section 2. Board of deacons.

The deacon's ordination is for life, or during the maintenance of Christian character, but he holds office at the pleasure of the church. Each deacon shall be an active member of the church and able and willing to participate in the affairs of the church. Deacons serve for a period of two years and may be re-elected.

The deacons shall be men distinguished among their brethren for soul-winning, visitation, piety, and benevolence. Their wives and children shall conform to the teachings of 1 Timothy 3:11 and 12. No man shall be put on trial for a deacon or ordained as a deacon who is not a soul-winner, who has ever at any time been divorced, who does not practice tithing, or who uses tobacco, drugs, or alcohol. If a deacon's wife shall pass away, it shall not affect his standing if he shall marry again. A candidate for this office, after having been on trial for a period of one year and by a vote of the church, shall be examined by the quarterly meeting or association of which this church is a member.

Until the church becomes a member of such an organization, an examining council shall be chosen by the church to examine him. The church shall uphold the decision of the examining council, and the candidate shall be properly ordained by at least three ordained men, with the pastor serving as chairman of the ordaining council.

If for any reason a deacon shall find himself unable to serve the church to the best of his ability, it shall be his duty to request the church to put him on the inactive list of deacons. This means that all power vested in the deacon by the church shall be removed until he shall find himself once again able to do what is required of him. If he shall fail to ask the church to place him on the inactive list, it shall be the privilege of a majority vote of the church, after attempting to provoke him to be active and correct his example, to place him on the inactive list of deacons.

It shall be the duty of the deacons to work under the direction of the pastor, and to be of assistance to the pastor, when needed, in the oversight of the work of the church. They shall be charged with the following responsibilities.

1. Soul-winning, both personal and through the visitation and outreach ministries of the church, shall be their duty.
2. The spiritual advancement and interest of the church and the watchcare of its members shall be their duty under the direction of the pastor.
3. The preparation and observance of the Lord's supper and feet washing services and assisting the pastor when needed in baptismal services shall be their duties.

4. The filling of the pulpit if it is vacated by the loss of a pastor shall be their responsibility.

5. The visiting and comforting of the sick, unsaved, and prospects shall be duties of the deacons.

6. Assisting the pastor, when needed, in seeing that efficient Scriptural discipline be enforced among the members is the responsibility of the deacons.

7. They shall serve as the nominating committee for the annual election of church officers.

8. They shall have meetings when called by the pastor. If a deacon feels the need of a special meeting, he shall request the pastor to call it.

9. They shall serve as the pulpit committee for the election of a pastor.

10. They shall keep the active membership list current. (See Article III, Section 7, 8, and 9.)

New deacons and deacons coming into the fellowship of this church, having been previously ordained in other Free Will Baptist churches, shall not be considered active deacons until after at least a twelve months' waiting period in the church and after a vote of the church.

The pastor and deacons shall decide when another deacon is needed and shall recommend the prospective deacon to the church to be put on trial.

Section 3. Clerk.

The clerk shall be an active member who attends faithfully all the regularly scheduled services of the church, soul-winning, and visitation. It is the duty of the church clerk to work under the direction of the pastor, and to keep accurately the records and minutes of all church business which shall be approved at each regular church business meeting. He shall keep a correct register of the membership with the date and manner of all admissions or dismissals, baptismal records, and other pertinent information. The clerk shall submit a report of the membership if necessary, not only to the church, but also to the district, state, and national associations as voted by the church.

The clerk shall sign all official communications made by the authority of the church along with the pastor. The clerk shall regularly submit a copy of all minutes of church business meetings to the pastor. He shall preserve in a safe place all church records and papers, making all reports in duplicate and submitting one copy to the pastor. He shall within two weeks after the annual meeting turn over to the newly elected clerk all records in his custody.

Section 4. Treasurer.

The treasurer shall be an active member who attends faithfully all the regularly scheduled services of the church, soul-winning, and visitation. It is the duty of the treasurer to work under the direction of the pastor, and to disburse all funds for local expenses, benevolences, and worldwide outreach ministries. He shall hold all monies belonging to the church, promptly depositing them in the bank to the account of the church, and shall without special vote of the church pay out of these funds all fixed monthly items. He shall pay all others only after they have been approved by the pastor or church. The treasurer and at least one other person shall co-sign all checks. He shall keep a record of all receipts and disbursements with proper vouchers. He shall print a monthly financial statement showing all offerings and receipts, the disbursements for the month, and the total in all accounts, and shall distribute copies to the membership.

He shall give both an oral and a printed summary of the financial condition of the church at each regular business meeting, and a complete itemized report at the annual business meeting, and at any other time the church may request it. He shall preserve in a safe place all church documents and legal papers. He shall make all his reports in duplicate, and submit one copy to the pastor. The outgoing treasurer shall within two weeks after the annual conference turn over to the newly elected treasurer all money, checks, books, records, and papers of the church in his custody.

Section 5. Music director, pianist, and organist.

The music director, pianist, and organist shall be active members who attend faithfully all the regularly scheduled services of the church, soul-winning, and visitation. They shall be elected by the church at the annual business meeting. They shall perform the duties required by the office which they hold. The membership of the church shall cooperate with the music director in the musical program of the church. The music director shall cooperate with the pastor in planning the musical program of the church and shall work under his direction.

Section 6. Board of trustees.

There shall be a board of trustees consisting of at least three members. They shall be active members who attend faithfully all the regularly scheduled services of the church, soul-winning, and visitation. They shall work under the direction of the pastor and shall hold in trust the property of the church, execute all deeds, debentures, mortgages, liens, transfers, leases, and other legal documents for and on behalf of the church, but shall have no power to buy, sell, mortgage, lease, transfer, or incumber any property of the church without the church authorizing such action.

They shall have charge of the upkeep of all property of the church. They shall be elected to serve for a period of two years, and may be re-elected. They shall preserve in a safe place all church documents and legal papers. They shall make all reports in duplicate, and submit one copy to the pastor.

Section 7. General Sunday school superintendent.

The general Sunday school superintendent shall be an active member who attends faithfully all the regularly scheduled services of the church, soul-winning, and visitation. He shall work under the direction of the pastor to exercise general oversight over all departments of the Sunday school and shall report to the church at its business meetings.

He shall see that the Sunday school operates under its own separate constitution and bylaws, making sure that accurate records are kept and submitted regularly to the pastor and church. The departmental superintendents shall direct the work of their respective departments subject to the oversight of the general superintendent. The general superintendent shall serve as chairman of the Christian education committee.

Section 8. Church Training director.

The Church Training director shall be an active member who attends faithfully all the regularly scheduled services of the church, soul-winning, and visitation. He shall work under the direction of the pastor and shall have general oversight of the work of all departments of the Church Training. He shall report to the church at its business meetings. He shall see that the Church Training operates under its own separate constitution and bylaws, making sure that accurate records are kept and submitted regularly to the pastor and the church. He shall be a member of the Christian education committee.

Section 9. Auditing committee.

The pastor at each annual business meeting shall appoint an auditing committee of three members whose duty shall be to work under the direction of the pastor, and to make a full examination of the treasurer's books, financial records, accounts, and vouchers of all officers having charge of the church funds, and to render a statement in writing at the end of each church year. They shall submit all reports in duplicate, giving one copy to the pastor.

Section 10. Ushers committee.

The ushers committee shall consist of a sufficient number and shall be appointed by the pastor. They shall work under his direction to collect the offerings and assist the pastor in welcoming visitors to the church. They shall secure seats and hymnals for all who need them and shall have charge of the heating, cooling, and ventilation of all rooms during the services. They shall give assistance in the parking of cars and church buses when needed.

Section 11. Christian education committee.

The Christian education committee shall be composed of at least three members of which the general Sunday school superintendent is chairman. The Church Training director shall also be a member of this committee. The committee shall work under the direction of the pastor and with the Sunday school department superintendents and teachers, and Church Training group leaders to promote Christian education in the church. The pastor and Christian education committee shall appoint all Sunday school officers and teachers, and all Church Training officers and group leaders. The pastor and Christian education committee shall have the authority to replace any Sunday school and Church Training teacher or worker who becomes unwilling or unable to fulfill his duties. They shall use as the guide for their work the standard of achievement for the Sunday school, the worker's covenant, and the constitutions and bylaws of the Sunday school and Church Training. Members of this committee, other than the general Sunday school superintendent and Church Training director, shall be appointed by the pastor.

Section 12. Advisory board.

There shall be an advisory board of the church consisting of the following: pastor, deacons, trustees, clerk, treasurer, music director, general Sunday school superintendent, and Church Training director, and also three members elected by the church. This board shall work under the direction of the pastor and shall meet at least once each quarter, before the regular business meeting, to consider the general work of the church. The work of this board shall be advisory in nature and character, except as otherwise provided by special vote of the church. All matters of vital importance should be presented to the advisory board before action is taken by the church. Seven members of the board shall constitute a quorum.

Section 13. Additional officers and staff members.

All other officers or associates to officers, and staff members who are to be elected by the church, shall perform such duties as their office requires and shall work under the direction of the pastor who shall determine their duties, and shall be subject to the pastor and the church. They shall be active members who attend faithfully all the regularly scheduled services of the church, soul-winning, and visitation. This would include associate pastors, bus ministers, youth ministers, ministers of Christian education, visitation ministers, music ministers, secretaries, janitorial workers, and any others the church sees necessary to employ.

Article VII

Meetings

Section 1. The Lord's day.

The church shall meet regularly on each Sunday morning and evening for public worship.

Section 2. Midweek service.

At least once each week the church shall meet for midweek prayer, Bible study, and public worship services.

Section 3. Soul-winning and visitation.

The church shall carry on a program of weekly soul-winning and visitation to reach the lost for Christ, and to contact prospects and absentees.

Section 4. Outreach ministries.

The church shall conduct outreach ministries as the need arises and as finances permit. These shall consist of a bus ministry, day care program, Christian schools, deaf ministry, radio and television ministries, literature and tract distribution ministry, evangelistic services in nursing homes, jails, rescue missions, and other Bible-based ministries that will reach the lost for Christ.

Section 5. Business meetings.

A quarterly business meeting shall be held by the church on a weeknight two weeks before the quarterly meeting of which the church is a member. Items of business may be transacted at any regular meeting of the church if an announcement of the intended action has been made at a previous regular meeting. The church shall have an annual business meeting on a weeknight two weeks before the annual associational meeting of which the church is a member. All necessary elections shall be carried out and all necessary reports shall be given at this meeting.

Section 6. The ordinances.

The Lord's supper and feet washing shall be observed at least once each year and may be as often as desired by the church or pastor. Baptismal services shall be as often as the need requires.

Section 7. Evangelistic meetings and missionary conferences.

Special evangelistic meetings, revivals, missionary conferences, and other such meetings shall be conducted as often as deemed necessary. They shall be arranged by the pastor.

Section 8. Special meetings.

Special meetings may be called by the pastor whenever he sees the need. A special meeting may also be called by ten active members over twenty-one years of age. It shall be necessary for the ten members to state in writing the reason for the meeting. The purpose for the meeting must be announced at a preceding worship service.

Article VIII

Auxiliary Organizations

Section 1. Affiliation.

All auxiliary organizations of this church shall be subject to the control of the church, and failure to work in harmony with the church shall be cause for disbanding such organization. No auxiliary organization shall meet during any regular worship service or during the weekly soul-winning and visitation programs of the church.

Section 2. Major organizations.

The Sunday school, Church Training Service, Master's Men, and Woman's Auxiliary shall be considered as major auxiliary organizations and shall function under their own separate constitutions and bylaws. Such constitutions and future amendments thereto shall be approved by the advisory board of the church and must be in harmony with the church constitution and bylaws.

Article IX

Church Buildings

Section 1. Description.

The church buildings shall be used for such meetings as will accomplish the purpose set forth in Article I, Section 2.

Section 2. Use.

The church buildings shall be available to church auxiliaries for fellowship meetings, class meetings, and other functions, providing that said meetings do not conflict with any regular scheduled service or soul-winning program of the church. The groups sponsoring the meetings shall assume full responsibility of cleaning the building after the meetings. All such meetings must be cleared with the pastor and with the church calendar. No meetings of any kind shall be held in the church buildings of which the pastor is not aware.

Section 3. Special use.

In case of an individual desiring the use of the church buildings for any purpose, he shall present a written application to the pastor.

Article X

Finance

Section 1. Method.

The financial support of this church shall be by personal, voluntary giving of tithes and offerings as an act of worship.

Section 2. Distribution of funds.

In case of special occasions involving the distribution of funds not otherwise provided for, the pastor, treasurer, and any two members of the board of trustees shall constitute a committee to decide upon such distribution. The pastor shall be allowed up to $_____ per month for necessary items not otherwise provided for without having to previously bring the matter to the advisory board or to the church. All checks must be co-signed by the treasurer and at least one other person.

Section 3. Denominational support.

This church shall contribute at least ten percent of its income to the support of the overall work of the denomination. This money shall be divided among the mission boards, Bible colleges, departments, and other enterprises as the church shall see fit. This ten percent shall be regarded as a minimum of the giving, and not a maximum.

Article XI

General

Section 1. Voting body.

All active members of this church above _____ years of age are
eligible to vote in all business meetings.

Section 2. Quorums.

In all regular business meetings one-fourth of the active
membership shall constitute a quorum. In the event of special
meetings for important matters such as   calling a pastor, sale or
purchase of property, or assumption of financial responsibility
by the church, then two-thirds of the active members shall be
necessary for a quorum.

Section 3. The will of the church.

The will of the church on any given matter duly expressed by
its vote, shall be carried out by all committees, officers, and
organizations of the church. When the church by majority vote
decides on any matter, each member must consider such action
as authoritative above his own personal opinion and shall accept
and abide by the decision.

Section 4. Manner of conducting business.

All business shall be conducted according to *Robert's Rules of
Order.*

Section 5. Licensing and ordaining of candidates for the ministry.

Licensed ministers must abide by the terms stated on their license. No man shall be licensed or ordained by this church who is not a soul-winner, who has at any time been divorced, who does not practice tithing, or who uses tobacco, alcohol, or drugs. The candidate shall pass the following written examination before this church shall be obligated to grant him license.

1. What has been your past experience and success in soul-winning? Give in detail your philosophy of soul-winning, visitation, and church growth.

2. Are you called of God to the ministry? Give a detailed account of that calling.

3. Do you believe it possible for man to make shipwreck of his faith and be lost after he has been truly converted? Why or why not?

4. Do you believe in open communion? Why or why not?

5. Do you believe in feet washing as a gospel ordinance? Why or why not?

6. Define the Scriptural method of water baptism. In whose name are we to baptize? Do Free Will Baptists baptize by sprinkling or immersion? Why?

7. Do you believe that water baptism is essential to conversion? Why or why not?

8. On what conditions do we accept members?

9. What duties can an ordained minister perform that a licensed minister cannot?

10. Do you believe in sanctification as a second definite work of grace? Why or why not?

11. Does a person receive the Holy Spirit at conversion, or is it a second work of grace? Why?

12. What is your explanation of the passage of Scripture in Acts chapter 2 in regard to speaking in other tongues?

13. Do you believe there are Christian people in churches other than Free Will Baptists?

14. Do you believe that men everywhere apart from Christ, including the heathen, are lost?

15. Is Hell eternal? Why or why not?

16. What must one do to be saved? Give in detail.

17. What are your plans to better qualify and prepare yourself for the ministry as far as schooling, Bible study, practical work in soul-winning and church growth methods?

18. What are the feelings of your family members as to your entering the ministry?

A licensed minister coming to this church from another church must pass the same examination as a candidate from this church. If he does not, this church is under no obligation to honor his license.

This examination shall be given by the ordained men of this church and they in turn will report to the church and offer their recommendations.

In order to qualify for ordination, he must serve at least one year on license, have shown evidence of study and improvement, and have work that requires ordination.

Article XII

Disposition of Church Property

Section 1. Organic division of the church.

In the event of organic division of the church membership, the church property shall belong to those members who abide by this constitution and bylaws and *A Treatise of the Faith and Practices of the Original Free Will Baptists.*

Section 2. Dissolution clause.

Should a condition arise at any time in the future when, for any reason, the church work cannot continue, making it necessary for the church to disband, the ownership of the church property, buildings, equipment, and funds shall be transferred to the Home Missions and Church Extension Board of the

National Association of Free Will Baptists, 1134 Murfreesboro Road, Nashville, Tennessee 37217.

Bylaws

1. No person should hold more than two offices in this church at one time, and preferably only one.

2. All officers of this church, with the exception of the pastor, deacons, and trustees, shall be elected at the beginning of each church year. A previous term in office does not exclude any person from being reelected.

3. Any person wishing to resign from his office in this church shall notify the pastor of such intentions as quickly as possible.

4. The pastor has the right to fill any office that is vacant by appointment until the church can meet to elect someone to fill the vacancy.

5. All eligible members of this church shall be expected to vote on all issues one way or the other. Voting shall be by secret ballot when it regards any ordained person. The pastor shall decide if the vote on other issues is to be an oral vote, a standing vote, by secret ballot, or a vote by raising of hands.

6. All delegates representing this church in any way shall be elected by the church when in business meeting. Proxies may be appointed by the pastor.

7. This constitution and bylaws may be amended at any
regular or called conference or business meeting of the
church by a majority vote of the body, provided that
fifty-one percent of all active members are present, and
provided that the intended amendment be announced at a
preceding meeting of the church. The amendment must be
in writing and tabled until the next meeting.

The church planter should have the constitution and
bylaws ready when he begins services. He should test it in the
early weeks and months before the church is organized, making
sure it is just the way he wants it. Then prior to organizing the
church, he should distribute copies to the prospective members,
and after they have studied it sufficiently, meet together and
adopt it. It should be changed, deleted, and added to as each
local church sees fit.

Incorporation and Tax Exemption

The first few weeks after services are begun, the church
should file for incorporation as a nonprofit corporation with
the state. The church does not need a lawyer for this. The
National Home Missions Department has on file the requirements for incorporation in any state, or the church planter can
contact the office of the Secretary of State at the state capitol,
and this office will send the forms which anyone can fill out,
giving the name of the church, its purpose, and the signatures of
either three or five members, depending upon the state's
requirements.[7]

It is important for a church to incorporate because it is

then listed in the state as a nonprofit organization. This makes the contributions of its members tax-exempt. The Internal Revenue Service does not have to honor gifts to a church that is not incorporated as a religious nonprofit corporation.

Incorporation also insures that litigation matters would involve the church as a corporation and not individual members. Creditors could not take property or money by law from individual members as payment for the debts of the church.

Once the church is incorporated it should also file for a tax-exemption number. The forms can be obtained from the post office or a federal building. This number will be issued and can be used by the church in making its purchases so that it will not have to pay taxes. It will also take it off the property tax roll.[8]

Organizing the Church

The preacher should be anxious to organize the church, but he should not be too hasty. The church does not have to be organized to be incorporated, to obtain a tax-exempt number, or to buy property. It should be organized only when it is functioning as a Free Will Baptist church should function. Until that time it should remain unorganized, but it should never be called a "mission." From the very outset it should be referred to as a church.[9]

When Christ has done the work in the hearts of the people, and the pastor has taught them so they can properly function as a church, they are ready to be organized into a church. Therefore the organizational service is just recognition day.[10]

When time for the organization arrives, appropriate people

such as officials from the local, district, or state associations, and sponsoring mission boards and supporters should be notified. Organization should be a glorious time and supporters may want to be present for the service.

The constitution should be completed. A charter membership roster should be made up that will have accumulated names from the first service until the organizational service.[11] This will give the preacher a way to handle the situation of those wanting to join the church before it is organized.

A nominating committee should have completed its work. When the time for the organizational service arrives, the organizational council will set the church in order according to *A Treatise of Faith and Practices of the Original Free Will Baptists*, and receive the members who will then elect the pastor. The pastor will then ask the congregation to officially adopt the constitution and bylaws, elect church officers from the nominating committee's report, take care of any business, and dismiss the service for a time of refreshments and fellowship. A sample order of service follows.

Hymn
Prayer
Welcome
Organizational Message
Presentation of the Bible
Presentation of the *Treatise*
and Church Covenant
Organization of Church
Act of Dedication
Prayer of Dedication
Election of Pastor

Election of Church Officers
Adoption of Constitution and Bylaws
Miscellaneous Business
Prayer
Fellowship and Refreshments[12]

Some church planters combine the organizational service and the dedication of property and buildings. However, some churches may want to officially organize before acquiring property or going through building programs.

Denominational Affiliation

The local church, once organized, should affiliate itself with the National Association of Free Will Baptists by uniting with the appropriate associations within the state. In states where there is no district or state association as yet, this will mean joining the National Association as a local church. Associations should be organized in these areas when there are other churches to associate with in a fellowship.

The purpose of belonging to the National Association of Free Will Baptists is to enable the local churches to do together what they cannot do separately—support a worldwide missions and educational program—thus fulfilling the Great Commission, and for the purpose of fellowship.

The National Association of Free Will Baptists as a cooperative fellowship is a voluntary cooperation among independent churches. It is an association of free citizens, believers in local churches where fellowship exists among them. One church does not interfere with another. No super organization exists that seeks to impose its will on individual churches. There is democracy within the local church and the autonomy of the local church is protected in its relationship to other churches.

When individual churches join forces in a voluntary cooperation among independent churches they do not surrender their autonomy. In cooperative fellowships sincere men are attempting to more effectively minister the common core of doctrinal beliefs which bind them together. No super organization speaks authoritatively for all the churches. The local church is still self-determining and no hierarchy exists which hands down dictates. No church is stigmatized or relegated to a secondary status if it chooses not to support programs, and what a church gives does not become the criterion of orthodoxy. The churches are bound together with a fellowship and a like doctrine for more effectively accomplishing the work of Christ through literature programs, missions programs, educational programs and institutions such as Christian schools, Bible colleges, and institutes.

There are no disadvantages to a church being affiliated with the National Association of Free Will Baptists. The denomination does not have colleges or professors that have departed from the fundamentals of the faith. The church can proudly support any phase of the denominational work without compromise of doctrine or convictions.

The local church does not lose its autonomy to a denominational machine. The local church bears the entire cost of financing the buildings and property, and the deeds to the property are made out in the name of the local church.

Denominational cooperation does not cause churches to lose control of the election of their pastors. The pastor is not chosen for the church by a bishop, associational secretary, or denominational official. He is chosen by the vote of the local congregation itself.

A pastor can cooperate within a fellowship without spending countless hours and endless days on denominational agencies and institutions. What amount of time is spent in denominational meetings will result in times of refreshing, renewal, and challenge for the cooperating pastor.

Denominational cooperation is possible among independent New Testament churches under the lordship of Christ and whose sole rule of faith and practice is an authentic, authoritative, and infallible Bible. These churches can remain independent and self-determining.

It is possible to promote the gospel of Christ in fellowship with other pastors without entangling alliances. A fundamental pastor and church can cooperate with other fundamental pastors and churches without becoming part of an ecclesiastical system. Through such cooperation, there is no usurpation of the powers of the local church.

So the new church, once organized, should affiliate with the National Association of Free Will Baptists, send its pastor and delegates to its meetings, and support its causes. That way it will have a literature program of quality materials, Bible colleges to send its students for training, and national departments offering assistance in many areas.

Conclusion

Some pastors seem to be afraid of using a constitution and bylaws or having any organization in the church. If the pastor has carefully thought through the organizational structure of the church and written it into a constitution, it can help his church run more smoothly and eliminate many problems. It also establishes the continuation of the church's ministry after the church planter has left for other fields of service.

The questionnaire for licensing of ministers is included especially for churches in isolated areas where there is no associational examining committee. It is a good idea for any church to carefully screen its candidates for the ministry before licensing. Such a questionnaire will help.

Written procedures are always better than unwritten. If the church planter will think and pray carefully about the organizational structure of the church, he will set a frame work on the foundation from which the church can be built.

Chapter V
Reference Notes

[1]Elmer Towns, *Getting a Church Started in the Face of Insurmountable Odds with Limited Resources in Unlikely Circumstances* (Nashville: Impact Books, 1975), p. 131.

[2]Donald J. McNair, *Birth, Care, and Feeding of a Local Church* (Grand Rapids: Baker Book House, 1971), p. 124.

[3]Lee Lebsack, *Ten at the Top* (Stow, Ohio: New Hope Press, 1974), p. 11.

[4]*A Treatise of the Faith and Practices of the Original Free Will Baptists* (Nashville: Executive Office, National Association of Free Will Baptists, 1977), pp. 7-45.

[5]Max Helton, "A Constitution and By-Laws," (Hammond, Indiana: Helton Publications, n.d.).

[6]George Godfrey, *Helps to Have a Soul Winning Church*

(Crown Point, Indiana: Hyles-Anderson College, 1976), p. 121.

[7]Helton, "A Constitution and By-Laws."

[8]*Ibid.*

[9]Roy Thomas, *How to Start a Church from Scratch* (Nashville: Free Will Baptist Board of Home Missions, 1974), p. 10.

[10]Towns, p. 146.

[11]Helton, "A Constitution and By-Laws."

[12]Thomas, p. 11.

CHAPTER VI

FINANCES AND RECORDS

The financial program of any church is of extreme importance, but especially in a church just beginning. People are not acquainted with each other. They do not know those who receive and disburse the money. There is no property or buildings to give security. The church and denomination may be strange to those attending.[1]

The place to begin having a successful financial program for the church is with the pastor managing his personal finances. He will treat the church's money and conduct its business similar to the way he conducts his personal business.[2] It is extremely important that a new pastor moving to a city have a good financial record. Unpaid bills and a bad credit record will soon catch him and ruin his chances for a good ministry. People will not put money into a church where the pastor is a poor manager of his own money. Banks will refuse to make loans to a church with a pastor who has a poor credit rating. So the church planter must learn to live on his income and meet his obligations on time, thus establishing good credit ratings.

The Church Budget

The church planter will have prepared a temporary church budget which was distributed in his Tuesday night "get acquainted meetings" and to those attending the first service. This budget should begin with some money toward the pastor's salary. Even though the church planter may receive his salary from a mission board or other sources, he must begin immediately to train the church to pay the pastor's salary. The new church should begin by paying at least $100.00 per month toward the pastor's salary.[3] This amount should be increased as often as possible. If the pastor's salary could be increased by $100.00 per month, the new church could become self-supporting in one year. The pastor will have to take the lead in this matter and help the church increase its faith a step at a time. The pastor who fails in leading the church to assume the pastor's salary will defeat his own purpose. The church will not grow numerically or financially, and the church planter will make the sacrifice in the end because he will have to depend on a church he failed to train for his livelihood.

The church should include $100.00 per month in the budget for the pastor's salary and increase that amount by $25.00 each month. The first month the church would pay $100.00, the second month $125.00, the third month $150.00, and so forth. At the end of four years the church would be self-supporting and paying its pastor $1,275.00 per month, or $15,300 per year. The church planter must not let the need for property and buildings keep him from adopting a plan for assuming the pastor's salary.

The rent for the meeting place should be included in the church budget. By this time the church planter will know the amount that must be paid.

Some money should also be included for a building fund, so that the church can see the account build and the day approaching when property can be purchased. Special offerings may be taken and appeals made to help the building fund grow. It should be put in a savings account. The amount of $50.00 monthly could be put in the budget for this.

Some money should be put in the budget for office

supplies, as there will be many things the pastor will need, and the church needs to be trained to provide these items. The amount of $25.00 per month should be sufficient in the beginning.

If the church has a bus, it will cost about $90.00 per month to operate.[4] This should be included in the budget.

The amounts of $100.00 per month for advertising and $100.00 per month for promotion should be included in the budget. By advertising is meant newspaper ads, radio announcements, brochures, and printed materials to be distributed. The money in the budget for promotion could be spent on Bibles and other items used to reach people and secure their attendance.[5] One might think it better to put this $200.00 per month in the building fund. But the preacher will have to reach people if he builds a church. Unless he reaches the people, he will not need property and buildings. Once he gets the people, they will pay for the property and buildings. Twenty tithers can support a church. Ten tithers can support the pastor at their own average income level, and ten tithers can support the building payments and other expenses.[6]

Some money should be included for telephone expense. The church should be listed in the yellow pages of the telephone book in the church section as soon as possible. The pastor should insist that the church listing be worded as a "Free Will Baptist church" denoting it as a separate denomination, and not just another Baptist church, so it can be found easily. About $25.00 per month should be sufficient for telephone expense.

The budget should include $25.00 per month for postage, as the new church will need to do much promotion and follow up through the mail. Also $20.00 per month could be included for miscellaneous.[7]

The new church should begin by giving at least ten percent of its income to outside causes. One of the best ways for a church to teach its members to tithe is for the church itself to tithe. Naturally a new church cannot give as much before it has its own property, buildings, and pastoral support, as it can in later years, but it should begin by giving ten percent to outside causes. A portion of this should go to National Home Missions. The missionary who leads his church to support Home Missions shows the congregation that church planting as he is doing is important. The church should begin with a worldwide outreach. The outside giving should be held at ten percent until the church is self-supporting.[8]

The monthly budget suggested below could be adopted:

Pastor's salary	$100.00
Rent	150.00
Office supplies	25.00
Advertising	100.00
Promotion	100.00
Bus ministry	90.00
Telephone	25.00
Postage	25.00
Sunday school literature	35.00
Building fund	50.00
Miscellaneous	20.00
Outside giving	80.00
TOTAL:	$800.00

However, $25.00 per month will need to be added to this total to raise the pastor's salary on a graduated basis. This gives the new church a beginning budget averaging $862.50 per month for the first six months. The offerings will need to average approximately $200.00 per week to reach the budget.

The Offerings

Many problems church planters face have been in the area of church finances. Therefore, it is imperative that everything regarding finances be carefully planned and all records kept accurately.

One of the first things the missionary should do is appoint a treasurer. This should be a person who will attend all the services so the offerings can be obtained for deposit. The treasurer should be instructed to deposit the money in the bank in the church's accounts as quickly as possible. The treasurer should get a deposit slip which will correspond with the offering tally slip placed in the offering by those who count the money.

The treasurer should be provided with books to record offerings and expenditures. Each month a printed financial report should be distributed to all members stating the income and itemized expenditures for the month. A monthly accounting to the people is of utmost importance to encourage confidence in the new church.

The treasurer should be chosen with care. It should be someone outside the pastor's family. It should be a person who will not let what people give or do not give influence his attitude toward them. It should be a person who will recognize that the spending of the money is the church's decision, and he is just designated to keep accurate records and write the checks. Often treasurers can cause real problems because they look at the church money as if it were their own.

No pastor should ever sign checks or physically handle any of the funds. At least two signatures should be required on all checks. There could be three signatures accepted so that if one person is out of town, checks could still be written.[9]

The treasurer should be diligent and faithful to stub all checks as they are written and keep up on book work weekly. A slothful treasurer will trust to memory and catch the books up just before business meetings, which could result in a financial crisis for the church.

The treasurer should make reports at the church business meetings, annual reports at the end of each fiscal year, and keep the pastor posted at all times about the financial matters of the church.

Ushers are also important people when it comes to the matter of offerings. Not only are they the first people visitors meet, but they are also the first people to see the money given by the congregation.

The ushers should be taught to come down the aisles in an orderly fashion and receive the offering in a dignified manner. The offerings should be received from the front of the building, with the ushers facing the people, not from the back. No apologies should be made for receiving offerings. The pastor should emphasize the importance of giving. Receiving the offerings from the back could leave the impression that the pastor is embarrassed to receive offerings. People need to see the offering plates coming and prepare their offerings as acts of worship.

The offerings should be received as quickly as possible. As the congregation grows, another group of ushers can be added who can be stationed in the middle of the building, while the first group starts in the front. Enough time should be given, however, for people to write their checks.

When the offering is received it should be deposited in a place where no one can get to it while the preaching is in progress. If there is not a place in the building where it can be locked, then it should be brought back to the front and placed on the communion table or inside the pulpit. An incident of stealing from the church offering will destroy the confidence of the people and affect their giving.

It is very important that there be very tight control systems for counting the money. There should be persons designated to count the offerings at the close of the services and include tally slips with the totals in the offerings. This will help the treasurer to be assured that he also has counted correctly before making deposits. A duplicate copy of each tally slip should be given to the pastor. The deacons, the ushers, or the trustees could be the counters designated. But at least two men should be present at every counting of the offering. The money should never be counted during services. The counters should be rotated so that the same people do not count every week, and the pastor should not count the money.

A committee of at least three persons should be chosen to audit the treasurer's books at least once each year and report its findings to the church. This is important for the protection of the treasurer and will give confidence to the people.

The mission church should provide its people with offering envelopes so that a record can be given them for their contributions. The Internal Revenue Service prefers a statement from the church to donors instead of cancelled checks, as one could give a check for an amount and take change from the offering. Offering envelopes can be ordered in bulk from the

Sunday School Department so that the people will have them to make their gifts. A copy of the church budget and a box of offering envelopes should be included in all membership orientation packets, and a thorough explanation of giving procedures should be made to all prospective members.

Record sheets for contributions can be ordered from the Sunday School Department. These have four copies with carbon on the back. What is recorded on the top sheet goes on the other three copies. Thus the contributions of an individual can be recorded, and at the end of each quarter he can receive a record of his offerings. The fourth copy can be used for his income tax records. This procedure requires the use of envelopes or checks, but will greatly increase the offerings and eliminate misunderstandings about the amount an individual has given in a year's time. It will also give the contributor confidence in the church, the missionary pastor, and his financial program.

The home missionary pastor should set the example by being a faithful, consistent tither. Hammering away on tithing from the pulpit is not the best way to make tithers of the people. Sermons on tithing may be necessary on rare occasions, but if the people can be taught at other times, it will not give visitors the impression that the church is interested only in their money. The Home Missions Department's *Follow Up Lessons for New Converts to Christ* have a lesson on tithing. A training class for new converts is one of the best places to make tithers of people. A stewardship campaign each year will also greatly help in making tithers of the people.

The Stewardship Program

Once the pastor has the preliminary financial arrangements

made, he should begin building a solid financial program for the church. The place to start is by building confidence. Every pastor must develop and earn the confidence of his people if he is going to build a strong financial program. He does this by " . . . providing things honest in the sight of all men" (Romans 12:17).[10]

There should be a thorough and honest accounting by the church of the manner in which it disburses its funds. Failure to provide mechanisms for systematic disclosure of finances gives opportunity for criticism.[11] This can be done in several ways. An annual audit should be made. No bank would consider a large loan to a church that does not have its books audited annually. In the beginning, the audit can be taken by a committee from the church, but when the church grows large enough, a professional audit should be made.

A stewardship committee could be used to help prepare the budget, arrange for the stewardship campaign, and watch over the financial program of the church. The treasurer should be a member. The deacons could be this committee.

A printed monthly financial report of the church income and expenditures should be given the people, and a quarterly report of their individual contributions should be given or mailed. There should be no activity that would suggest that the money is spent wastefully. The pastor should make sure that designated funds are spent for the reason they are given.[12]

Many pastors suffer from the illusion that their people have no money. The people have money and they will tithe if properly encouraged and taught. The problem with lack of finance has less to do with external circumstances than with pastoral leadership. The Lord and the people are the church's only assets. She must look to them for her financial needs.[13]

The Stewardship Campaign

The church planter should begin the new year with a stewardship campaign. The preparation for the campaign should begin with the planning of the budget. As time progresses the budget should be enlarged to include property and building payments. Preliminary work on the budget should start in October so that the necessary time can be spent to have it ready by January 1.[14] Income and expenses for the year to date should be carefully studied by the pastor. He should draw up sheets for the stewardship committee with the various items listed. He may list some new items and the committee may see some items which need to be added.[15]

A budget is a forecast of anticipated activities and future needs, so it should reflect both sound judgment and faith.[16] The pastor and committee will be wise to spend some time and real prayer on the budget. A good rule to follow is to be conservative when anticipating income, and be realistic in anticipating expenses.[17]

The budget should be broken down into monthly and weekly figures.[18] The portion of the pastor's salary the church will assume that year should be broken down and included in the monthly budget. The church should be paying more by the end of the year than at the beginning.

When the committee has the budget ready, it should be presented to the advisory board for approval. Then copies should be given to the church membership for study. In December the church should vote to adopt the budget for the coming year. Once the budget is adopted, items within the budget may be spent without the vote of the church.[19]

Once the budget is adopted the pastor should begin the

stewardship campaign. Special stewardship lessons should be prepared for the Sunday school classes. There should be three lessons taught the first three weeks of January to all the Sunday school on stewardship. The pastor may want to preach some sermons on the subject. He must have a good positive sermon on tithing to preach in the Sunday morning service before the stewardship banquet which could be held on the last Friday night in January or another suitable night.

The pastor should prepare a series of letters to be mailed out each week in January. These letters will need to be about giving, about goals of the church, about the budget, and about the banquet.

During stewardship month, lessons could also be prepared for CTS classes, and special ministries of the church could be presented on Wednesday nights.

The banquet should be held at the church's expense. There should be a nice meal and a good speaker to challenge the people. Every effort should be made to have all the people present. Activities should be planned for the children elsewhere so the adults can concentrate on the information. At the climax of the banquet, commitment cards should be given for the people to put the estimated amount they will give to the church the next year. The cards should be unsigned with the information each person puts on the card remaining secret.[20] Such a stewardship campaign will gain new tithers for the church and put the church in good financial condition.[21]

The Records

It is so important for a church to keep good records. In order to do so, the necessary supplies should be obtained.

The church should provide offering envelopes for the people to enclose their contributions and drop in the offering plate. These could be distributed at the stewardship banquet. As people unite with the church during the year, packets of offering envelopes could be given them in their membership orientation packets. Extra offering envelopes should be available to the people in the church at all times.[22]

There should be a summary of receipts or tally slips provided for the counting committee to assist them in recording the offerings. One copy should be enclosed with the offering for the treasurer and another copy kept on file at the church for the pastor.[23]

The treasurer should be provided with a cash receipts journal to record the offerings for each week and a cash disbursements journal to record all disbursements. The building fund should be placed in a separate account with a separate set of record books.[24] The treasurer can also be provided with a financial statement book with sheets to assist in making weekly, monthly, quarterly, and annual reports to the church.[25]

Record of contribution forms are also very important to be used in sending quarterly and annual reports to individuals with a record of their contributions.[26]

The church should have one person who purchases for the church, which is usually the pastor in the beginning. He should fill out a purchase order for every item obtained. Teachers and others who need to obtain their own supplies should fill out purchase orders provided by the church.[27]

With these inexpensive record supplies the church can have a record of all money received and disbursed, and know exactly where it came from and how it was spent.

In addition to financial records, the church should

maintain records on prospects, visitors to the church, Sunday school and Church Training attendance, teacher and officer activities, visitation and soul-winning statistics, bus ministry records, legal and business transactions, a church history, plus any other records that become pertinent to the operation of a busy, enthusiastic church.[28]

There should also be needed supplies for the church clerk. A book to record the membership will be needed, and the clerk should be instructed to be present to get the information from those who make decisions in the services so proper action can be taken. Those who deal with people responding during the invitations should fill out decision cards, and files of this important information should be maintained. Those who unite with the church should be presented with membership orientation packets containing information concerning the church and all needed supplies. Membership cards should be obtained by the clerk on all joining the church, and from this needed information follow-up letters may be sent.

Request for church letter forms should be provided for the clerk, as well as forms for granting letters. The clerk should have a supply of baptismal and membership certificates to be presented to those who are baptized and join the church.

The clerk will also need a book in which to record the minutes of the business meetings. Also, proper forms will be needed to submit reports to the district, state, and national associations. These are provided by the National Executive office.

Good records help the pastor and church know what it has done, is doing, and what it plans to do. Records should always be honest, true, and promptly recorded so as to be accurate.

Conclusion

No part of the church work is more necessary than its financial program. The pastor should be honest in receiving offerings. When the offering is received and counted the people should know the total. No money should ever be spent for something other than what it was taken for.

Offerings could be taken on Wednesday night prayer meetings for such things as missions, building fund, bus ministry, or radio programs. All such offerings should go to the ministry thus designated.

The pastor should never conceal anything from the people, but keep everything honest and aboveboard. If he will be honest with them, he will build their confidence in his financial responsibility, and they will provide the money essential to a growing church.[29]

Chapter VI
Reference Notes

[1]Roy Thomas, *The Home Mission Church and Finances* (Nashville: Free Will Baptist Board of Home Missions, 1976), p. 1.

[2]Leslie Parrot, *Building Today's Church* (Grand Rapids: Baker Book House, 1973), p. 154.

[3]Thomas, p. 3.

[4]Jack Hyles, *The Hyles Church Manual* (Murfreesboro, Tennessee: Sword of the Lord Publishers, 1968), p. 96.

[5]Max Helton, "The Budget," (Hammond, Indiana: Helton Publications, n.d.).

[6]*Ibid.*

[7]Thomas, p. 3.

[8]*Ibid.*

[9]Hyles, p. 35.

[10]Truman Dollar, *How to Carry Out God's Stewardship Plan* (Nashville: Thomas Nelson Publishers, 1974), p. 36.

[11]*Ibid.*, p. 38.

[12]*Ibid.*, p. 41.

[13]*Ibid.*, p. 33.

[14]*Ibid.*, p. 81.

[15]Hyles, p. 29.

[16]Dollar, p. 33.

[17]Eugene C. Neithold, *Church Business Policies Outlined* (Greenville, South Carolina: Church Books, 1976), p. 42.

[18]Dollar, p. 82.

[19]Hyles, p. 29.

[20]Dollar, pp. 96-106.

[21]Charles M. Underwood, editor, *Planting the Independent Fundamental Church* (Greenville, South Carolina: Bob Jones University, 1972), p. 66.

[22]Dollar, p. 77.

[23]J. M. Crowe, *Church Finance Record System Manual* (Nashville: Broadman Press, 1959), p. 47. Used by permission.

[24]*Ibid.*, p. 40.

[25]*Ibid.*, p. 42.

[26]*Ibid.*, p. 46.

[27]*Ibid.*, p. 48.

[28]Underwood, p. 63.

[29]Hyles, p. 39.

CHAPTER VII

PROPERTY AND BUILDINGS

The church planter should always be watchful for suitable facilities for the new church to purchase so it can have a home of its own.[1] Having its own property and buildings will do several things for a church. The community will realize the church is permanent. The congregation will become part of the city as a property holder. The church identifies itself with the neighborhood when it purchases property. Permanent facilities allow the congregation to channel their energies into reaching people rather than preparing the building.[2]

Choosing a Site

An important item in building a new church is its location. Churches should be accessible. They should be on or near through streets and large arteries. They should not be buried in a housing development. It is a good idea to survey suitable sites from a small airplane. This will reveal if there are large industrial plants, forest preserves, or too many golf courses that take up land area and reduce the concentration of housing in a given location.[3]

First, the church planter must determine the section of the city or suburb he feels the Lord would have the church located. The church should go where the people are the most receptive to the gospel. It is not best to put the church in a Jewish, Catholic, or rich community. It should be in a section where working people live.[4] The price and value of homes, the economic level, and ethnic composition of the people should be learned.

The area to look for should be one with a high population of working-class people, with no growing fundamental church. It should be easily accessible from all parts of the city, which means that a corner location on two main arteries not far from a freeway is the most desirable location. The church planter should look for a desirable location, not just inexpensive land.[5]

Next it must be determined how much land should be obtained. The church should secure a minimum of five acres. If the church planter has a vision of a Christian school and a large multiministry church, he should try to obtain ten acres or more.[6] The possibilities of a radio ministry, a television ministry, a large bus ministry, children's clubs, and surplus parking should also be considered.[7]

The physical boundaries of the property will need to be checked. Railroads, roads, ravines, parks, golf courses, freeways, airports, industries, cemeteries, shopping centers, schools, and other establishments in the area must be taken into consideration.[8]

The elevation should be checked. It is good to locate a church on a hill where it can be seen. At any rate, the site should be high and dry so as not to be flooded during possible rainy seasons.[9]

Sometimes a piece of inexpensive land may be found, or someone may offer to donate a piece of ground. These temptations should be resisted if the site does not meet the needs of the new church.[10]

The opportunity to purchase an existing church may also be presented. If this is the best the church can do, naturally one must do what he feels is God's will. Although this is usually the most inexpensive route to take, it is not usually the best. The building will have been built for someone else's needs. It may have no baptistry, inadequate Sunday school facilities, and insufficient parking with no room for expansion. In an old building, repairs and utilities would be expensive. But the strongest reason against buying an existing church is that the new congregation would be moving into an area that the previous church or churches have already worked and abandoned.[11]

Before obtaining an option on prospective land, a feasibility study should be made so that the new church can be located in a place where it can grow, where nothing will hinder the construction of buildings or prevent the growth and expansion of the church. With a complete feasibility study, the church planter can go before the church with the assurance that he has checked every detail. This in-depth study will spare the church many problems if properly done. The following are many items that should be considered in such a study.

All adjacent property should be checked to determine what has happened in the area, what is happening, and what is about to happen. Land adjacent to nothing is always more economical than land adjacent to something. So extra land will be less expensive at the present than it will ever be again.

Noise factors from airlines, trains, and fast moving traffic should be checked. Too much noise can disrupt and interfere with services.

Possible odors should be checked. The smell of a nearby stockyard or gas refinery can send the prospective members to a church across town where the air is fresher.[12]

By going to the city planning commission, zoning laws and annexation proceedings may be obtained, along with water and sewer regulations and costs. Water rights should be checked to see if this is available to all parts of the property. Many times property only a certain distance from the street has water rights. Information should be obtained as to the costs and difficulty involved in connecting to sewer and water lines. The plumbing codes should be checked. Information should be obtained to see if the city sewer lines are available, or if a septic tank will have to be provided. This information will also determine if sewer lines have to be paid for even though not used.

Electrical requirements can be learned. If the wiring has to be run-in conduit, it can greatly affect the cost of wiring the buildings.

Investigation needs to be made to determine if title insurance can be obtained and if the buyer has to pay for the deed being brought up-to-date. It also will reveal if there are back taxes or other property taxes, and if there are any stipulations in the deed that would affect the building and operation of a church, a Christian school, or any other church related ministries. Also this investigation will determine the assessed value of the property.

A proper feasibility study will also determine if driveway, curb, and excavation permits can be obtained if required by the city. A soil test should be made. Ninety percent of locations will be suitable for building a church, but if a soil test reveals that the land may shift or swell, or pillars have to be sunk beneath the footings, it will make the building cost much more.

A check should be made into the local fire codes and how far away the nearest fire station is located. Investigation will reveal if there are fire plugs in the area. These things will affect the cost of insurance. Fire codes may also require fire dampers installed in each room. These could run into thousands of dollars in a church building. Also a check should be made concerning doors, to determine if solid core doors are required or even steel doors. This will greatly affect the cost of construction.

This study will also determine if a minimum square footage is required of church buildings. It will reveal the traffic flow, parking requirements per family in the congregation, paving costs, the costs of cutting streets through the property if there are none, and if there are existing or future plans to widen streets or put in sidewalks.

A check should be made as to what type of buildings can be built on the property and if buildings can be built before the land is paid for completely. Also, information should be obtained as to whether the church could later sell part of the land if it desired, and if there is a waiting period before any part of the land could be sold. A check should be made if there are any stipulations about to whom it can be sold. Investigation can determine if a deed can be obtained separate from the remainder of the land and thus allow for a mortgage so a building can be erected.

Road or street frontage should be determined, and also a check should be made to determine if property taxes must be paid on vacant land whether it is owned by a church or not. A check should be made to see if the parsonage will be tax-exempt if it is built on the church property. Drainage and engineering problems on the land should also be checked.[13]

The church can learn many things from the business world. The first thing a business man looks for is accessibility. He needs a good road to his place of business. The church will be better off near an interstate, accessible to all parts of the city than in a neighborhood or community.

Next, the business man wants surplus parking, not just ample parking, for those special days when he has a large crowd of customers. Some believe that surplus parking is the number one criterion in order for a church to grow.[14]

Generally, a competent Christian realtor can save the church both time and money since he is in a better position to know real estate values in a given area. Be sure to explain to him your present limitations, your future plans, and that an option or proposal on the property must be subject to approval by the governing body of your church and your attorney. It will probably be necessary to have this latter provision typed or written in, and it should be initialed by both parties.[15] Once the church planter, after careful investigation and much prayer, has settled on a piece of property, he should go after it.[16]

Financing of the Property

The beginning church should establish a building fund and allow it to grow as rapidly as possible, because the church will need some money to obtain land and put up a building. Many new churches use their building fund money to pay down on their property and then pay the land off as rapidly as possible. Once the land is clear, it will serve as collateral for a loan on the first unit of the building.

It is almost impossible for a church to secure total financing to include the cost of land, erection of a building, furnishings, and equipment. It is very difficult to get any lender to loan money when the church has no money to invest. Even if the church is successful in this regard, it is likely that the repayment schedule would be impossible to meet by a group that has been unable to raise any cash for the building up to that point. Neither will responsible lenders take into consideration the pledges of members, for they are not as interested in pledges as performance. Therefore, most lenders will require a financial statement of what the church has done and is doing. Most lending institutions limit their loans to two and one half times the annual income of the church. So for a church to borrow $50,000 they would have to have an annual income of $20,000. This makes it extremely difficult for new churches because their income is not sufficient to make them eligible for the size loan necessary to put them in their own building.

Just as lending agencies have rules, the wise pastor needs some guidelines about indebtedness. If the debt gets too heavy for the church to carry, it would be very easy for the pastor to conveniently be "called to another field" while the people are left to struggle for long bleak years. In an instance such as this the next pastor will of necessity make the financial sacrifice to pay for such lack of planning. The wise pastor will " . . . sit down first and count the cost lest he begin to build and not have sufficient to finish" (Luke 14:28).

The church should not be afraid of debt, but understand what debt is. Money should never be borrowed to the extent that it will whittle away the church's net worth. Never borrow money for utilities, gasoline, tires, or other things that will be gone when or before the debt is paid. This is a fundamental principle. Borrow money only for that which has collateral, nondepreciable value. That means that money should never be borrowed for radio or television time, for salaries, or for literature and supplies.

Money should never be borrowed to pay the interest on

debt. If the church cannot pay its present obligations, the worst thing it can do is make more obligations.

A church should not borrow more than can be amortized over a twenty year period. For a debt to be longer than twenty years will result in the church paying too much interest.

Before borrowing money the church should build up its income to the point it can make the payments.[17] Many churches step out on what they call "faith" to build buildings which they expect to bring in the people who will fill the offering plates to overflowing, only to discover that buildings do not bring people. The new facility may provide more space and nicer surroundings, but the task of outreach still remains the responsibility of the membership.

The church planter should not magnify buildings, but reaching people. The church should raise all the money it can, and the debt should be limited to one-fourth of its monthly income.[18]

Waldo Wenning, perhaps the foremost authority on church funding, said, "Raise men—lift them up! Inspire their spirits! And they will support your ever increasing cash needs."[19]

Types of financing available to churches fall into four categories. (1) The conventional loan is one which a savings and loan will make to the church. These are usually available only to churches in a well-established community where the church is well-known and has plenty of property as security for the loan. Conventional loans are almost impossible to secure by mission churches.

(2) Some of the stronger state mission boards have funds available for small loans to help new churches within their state. The Board of Retirement and Insurance of the National Association of Free Will Baptists has some funds available for

loans to churches.

(3) Often someone within the church or a friend of the church will have access to a large sum of money and would prefer to see it working for a church than being in some savings account somewhere.

(4) The most popular method of financing among new churches is church bonds. The National Association of Free Will Baptists sponsors a bond company called Executive Church Bonds, Incorporated to assist churches in financing buildings. Many people are glad to invest in church bonds because they receive a good return on their money and help build a church at the same time. There are also advantages to the church such as elimination of discount and loan costs. In a nondirected program where the bond company just prints the bonds and brochures, the charge is very low. A construction loan is unnecessary since the money is available as the bonds are sold. The repayment schedule begins at a low figure and graduates upward for the first five years to allow growth to meet the increased payments. If the church needs additional money later on, a "B" issue can be added to the bond program.[20]

The greatest asset the church has is its outreach program. If the church is reaching people for Christ, God will provide the money for the needed facilities.

The pastor must make sure that he has thoroughly explained the financial plans to the advisory board for their adoption and to the church for its adoption. He will certainly need the people to be with him through the tedious months of the building program and the long years of monthly payments. It is wise to have the church attorney check and verify all steps taken by the church. This could result in the church avoiding serious complications across the years.[21]

Erecting the Building

Once the site has been selected and the property purchased, the next thing that must be done is the securing of an
architect. Most large cities carry building codes which classify
churches as public buildings and require plans and specifications
be prepared by a state licensed architect with his stamp placed
on the plans in order for building permits to be granted.

There are five phases of services available by most
architects.

1. A schematic design is drawn to show the church what the
   new building will be like.

2. A design development which will determine materials and
   cost is provided.

3. A construction drawing which will provide the electrical,
   plumbing, heating, and construction specifications is
   supplied.

4. Contract-letting drawings are provided as copies to be
   given to contractors for their bids.

5. Supervision of the construction of the building until its
   completion is guaranteed.

Most churches use only the first three phases which result
in large savings.[22]

The church planter will need to put careful thought and
much prayer into the choice of the architect, because one that

will help the church can result in savings of thousands of dollars. The architect should be one who is familiar with the special functional requirements of the fundamental, evangelistic church regarding worship and Christian education. He should also be one that will major on simplicity and serviceability rather than being elaborate.

The building should be beautiful as well as practical. People run away from ugliness, but they are attracted by beauty. Beauty helps generate enthusiasm and also marshals enormous support.[23]

The church planter may want to get a master plan drawn of his entire proposed building complex. All too often because of lack of vision, lack of planning, and lack of property, the church has been stymied just when progress was reaching the point where the church was becoming a great center of evangelism.

Master planning should include several factors. A planning committee should be formed composed of the pastor and the most knowledgeable men about construction in the church. This would probably be the trustees or deacons. They would serve throughout the construction of the building, and be granted the authority from the church to make the decisions necessary to build the buildings.

Certain areas have greater potential than others, and wise planning will provide for the immediate as well as continuing needs of the church. The first phase will need to have an auditorium and educational space to allow the church to grow to about 150 to 200 people. By this time the church will be self-supporting and strong enough to erect additional space.

The set-back restrictions, contour of the land, and trees will largely determine immediate and future placement of buildings. This is why a master plan is so important. Little intelligent planning can occur without a master plan.[24]

The next step after the plans are drawn is to decide how the building will be built. Contractors have three types of agreements available. First is the turn-key job. Here the church simply signs the contract for a certain amount of money, and the contractor builds the building and turns it to the church when it is finished. Second is the cost plus ten percent plan which is self-explanatory. Third is a contract plus a percent of any savings the contractor is able to secure. On larger buildings this is sometimes attractive to contractors.[25]

An inexpensive way to build is for the church to serve as its own contractor and subcontract the work. If the pastor knows enough about construction where he can oversee the work and see that it is done right, he can get several bids on each area of work and then sign contracts with those who give the best bids. If he cannot do this for some reason, a competent carpenter could be hired to supervise the work.

When the church acts as the contractor, it often can get lower rates from subcontractors. Church members can be used to help with parts of the work they are qualified to do. This will cut the cost twenty to thirty percent, plus eliminate ten to fifteen percent for the contractor's fee. So the building can sometimes be built in this way for approximately half what a contractor would charge to erect it. Often the church can buy materials cheaper, and if they run out of funds, they can stop construction until more money is available.[26]

The pastor will need to make sure that all work is done right and that final payments are not made until the work has been completed, passed inspections, and lien wavers have been signed. He will also need to see that adequate insurance coverage is secured for the buildings while under construction and also after completion.

The construction should begin with a special ground breaking ceremony, and conclude with a dedication service.[27] The growing church will never get out of a building program for very long. When a congregation sacrifices to build an auditorium this tells the community that the preaching of the gospel is important.[28]

The building should be kept clean and in good repair. The sign should be neat and attractive, the yard mowed, and the shrubs trimmed. People get their first impression of the church by its outside appearance.

Inside, the building should be clean, with everything in place for every service. Visitors coming to an untidy church can be compared to company coming to a dirty house. It does not leave a good impression.

When things break, they should be repaired immediately. Light bulbs should be replaced as soon as it is discovered they are burned out. Floors should always be clean and the furniture dusted. The rest rooms and nursery especially should be spotless and well supplied. The pastor or some other responsible person should walk through the building before every service and make sure everything is ready before the people begin arriving.

When services are over, lights, organs, public address system, and other electrical equipment should be turned off. A lot of church money can be wasted simply because no one is responsible to flip switches. The buildings should be locked to give protection from vandals.

Conclusion

Finally, when the project is complete, the dedication is

over, and all eulogies have been exchanged, both pastor and people must realize that the building is not an object of worship. It is simply an avenue or vehicle through which the church can accomplish its mission in the world. It is here that the church assembles, sings, prays, worships, gives, fellowships, and seeks the salvation of the lost.[29] The congregation must realize that the building is not an end in itself, but a means to an end. Therefore, the congregation should go forth to reach the lost for Christ, fill that building, and proceed with the construction of more buildings. "Hammers are seldom silent in a growing church."[30]

Chapter VII
Reference Notes

[1]Elmer Towns, *Getting a Church Started in the Face of Insurmountable Odds with Limited Resources in Unlikely Circumstances* (Nashville: Impact Books, 1975), p. 156.

[2]Lee Lebsack, *Ten at the Top* (Stow, Ohio: New Hope Press, 1974), p. 37.

[3]Charles M. Underwood, editor, *Planting the Independent Fundamental Church* (Greenville, South Carolina: Bob Jones University, 1972), p. 70.

[4]Towns, p. 141.

[5]*Ibid..*, p. 83.

[6]Underwood, p. 71.

[7]*Ibid.*, p. 73.

[8]Lyle Wacker, *Church Extension Handbook* (Forest Park, Illinois: North American Baptist Missionary Society, n.d.), p. 7.

[9]Charles W. H. Scott and others, *The Modern Pioneer*

(Assemblies of God Home Missions Department, 1967), p. 9.

[10]*Ibid.*, p. 10.

[11]Roy Thomas, *How to Start a Church from Scratch* (Nashville: Free Will Baptist Board of Home Missions, 1974), p. 8.

[12]Jules Donald Jernigan, *Quest for the Rainbow* (Grand Rapids: Baker Book House, 1975), p. 7.

[13]Underwood, pp. 81-90.

[14]Robert Schuller, *Your Church Has Real Possibilities* (Glendale, California: Regal Books, 1974), pp. 19-22. Used by permission.

[15]Jernigan, p. 7.

[16]Lebsack, p. 10.

[17]Schuller, pp. 27-28.

[18]Jack Hyles, *The Hyles Church Manual* (Murfreesboro, Tennessee: Sword of the Lord Publishers, 1968), p. 44.

[19]Schuller, p. 29.

[20]Jernigan, p. 46.

[21]*Ibid.*

[22]Wacker, p. 8.

[23]Schuller, p. 77.

[24]Jernigan, p. 13.

[25]Hyles, p. 46.

[26]Wacker, p. 8.

[27]Hyles, p. 44.

[28]Towns, p. 156.

[29]Jernigan, p. 46.

[30]Lebsack, p. 16.

CHAPTER VIII

WORKERS AND STAFF

If the church planter is to be successful, he must enlist other people in helping with the work. There must be teachers, visitation workers, deacons, ushers, trustees, and others who will volunteer their services and render their talents in the building of the church.

The church will be made up of both old and new Christians, in all likelihood. The new Christians will follow the pastor's leadership and enable him to build a church without friction, if properly led. Older Christians are not always malcontents simply because they attend a new church, but many times are good people who have been praying for a Free Will Baptist church to be established in their city. The church needs to be built on both old and new Christians. The new converts will add the zeal which a new church needs, while the established Christians will add stability and endurance.[1]

Standards for Workers

The new church will need to choose its workers with care. It is impossible to lead a church past its leaders. The pastor should appoint qualified people as they become available to fill the various positions and expand his core of workers as the need arises and qualified people become available. These people must share the pastor's philosophy and uphold his standards.

The teaching of standards is the duty of the pastor, especially in a new church. He must teach by precept and example what is required of the saints. The pastor must be firmly convinced in his own convictions and sure they are Biblically sound. Many times cultural or traditional standards will also have to be taught for the sake of Christian testimony. The standards should be set high, but the pastor should remember that he is not dealing with angels, but men. He must remember that he is in the business of building people. He should maintain high standards and expect them to be observed, but must be patient, endeavoring always to build up offenders in faithfulness.[2]

If the officers, workers, and leaders maintain the standards of the church, it will characterize the church as observing those standards. The rest of the church will follow the leaders, which will result in a united church and a clean, holy congregation.

In the beginning, before qualified workers are found, the pastor may teach the adult class and his wife a children's class. Later, qualified workers can be added as they become available. It is much easier to get standards from the beginning than to try to add them later.

In these days of new styles and fads, a church needs to adopt a dress code that will set a standard for men and women in places of leadership. This is in no way to impose legalism upon the people, but rather exhorts all to be examples of the believers. People in places of leadership should set the example for the rest to follow.

People in leadership include the pastoral and office staff, wives and families; deacons and their wives and families; church officers, Sunday school staff, choir members, and those who in any way contribute to the services, including ushers and any other helpers.

The Bible exhorts His people not to be conformed to this

world in Romans 12:1 and 2. The carnal, sensuous look of the world has no place in the house of God. The standard of dress should be one appropriate for Christian men and women.

Men should consider hair length as a very important part of their testimony, keeping the length of their sideburns moderate and avoiding the "mod" or "hippie" look with respect to hair over the ears and over the collar. It is expected that all men in any place of responsibility or leadership should have on a coat and tie while performing their responsibilities.

The women already mentioned are requested to give careful regard to skirt length, keeping the hemline no shorter than knee length. No one should participate on the platform unless her skirt length conforms. The attitude of the world toward women wearing slacks causes every church to have to face this problem. Women leaders of the church should set the example by wearing dresses to all worship services. The ladies should be ladies at all times and help set a standard for young girls.

Because of the teachings of 1 Corinthians 8:9-13 regarding the Christian's influence on the lives of others, people in places of leadership in the church are expected to live lives separated from the world. This includes abstinence from gambling, drinking alcoholic beverages, the use of tobacco and drugs, attendance at Hollywood movies, dancing, and any other questionable worldly amusements and activities.

The church leaders should set the example in faithful attendance at all services and participation in visitation and soul-winning activities. In their homes they should exemplify Christian standards in the training of their children, daily devotions, and family altars. In their personal lives they should stay close to the Lord through consistent Bible reading and prayer.

The church planter will do well to gather about him a group of workers who share his convictions and standards. This group will teach these standards by precept and example, and the church will follow their leadership.

Recruiting Workers

The pastor must use discretion when appointing church leaders. Often people want positions they are not qualified to fill. They may lack ability and talent, or be so emotionally unstable they would create chaos anywhere they might be placed.

Of course, the pastor needs to search his own heart and make sure he views the situation objectively, staying in tune with God, following His leadership in the choice of leaders for the church. All leaders will need to be appointed by the pastor in the beginning. As the church grows, deacons are chosen and an advisory board is formed. The pastor then should begin to work with them in the choice of leaders.[3]

A church produces its own leaders by getting laymen involved. A pastor who knows how to put people to work will have a happy, growing, excited church. The pastor who tries to suppress leadership and insists on doing everything himself may find that he must struggle constantly to keep down opposition.[4]

The pastor who can manage to have a good, friendly working association with his officers will find that it has eliminated most of his church problems. There must be a state of mutual respect between the pastor and the officers of the church. The entire church suffers when friction exists among the church officers, and the entire church progresses when harmony prevails.[5]

If the pastor will preach the Word, it will equip people to serve and will cause the ineligible to drop by the wayside. It is usually unwise to advertise to fill needed positions. Often the wrong people will volunteer and place the pastor in a precarious position.[6]

Workers should be recruited individually. They should not be "hounded" about standards after they go to work at the job, but should be talked to on a personal basis, with the standards of the church and the requirements of the position clearly defined beforehand.[7]

The pastor should pray for workers constantly and observe the congregation for an answer to his prayer. When he sees a person who is teachable and faithful and wants to be of service, he should decide the position the person is best suited for, and then approach him personally about it. The pastor should define the position and what it would require of him, explain the standards for workers, and ask him to pray about it.

In a week or two he should approach the person again to get his response. If the response is favorable, the candidate should be given a copy of the workers' covenant to read and pray over. After a few days the pastor should ask if the candidate has studied the covenant, and answer any questions he may have. The covenant may need to be read with the candidate to make sure everything is clear. If he agrees to the covenant, the pastor should proceed to place him in the position desired.[8]

How a person is recruited has a lot to do with how he will serve. People should not be recruited on the street, in the parking lot, or in the aisle of the church.[9] The pastor should invite candidates to his office or call and make appointments to go to their homes and personally lay the challenge before them.[10]

The pastor should be constantly watching his congregation for those the Lord will raise up as leaders in answer to his prayers. He should pour his life into young men, training them, taking them on visitation, making soul-winners out of them. These will be some of the best workers in the church.[11]

The pastor should include in his invitation on occasion an appeal for dedication to Christian service. When people make a public decision about the bus ministry or soul-winning, they usually will stick with that decision.

A church workers' covenant is a valuable tool in recruiting workers. It establishes the standards required of workers. Each worker will know exactly what is expected of him. In case he does not live up to the standards, he can be shown that he is not fulfilling his part of the agreement.[12]

The following is a sample workers' covenant.

Realizing the importance, privilege, and responsibilities of the ministry of the_____Free Will Baptist Church:

I HEREBY DECLARE:

1. That I have accepted Jesus Christ as my personal Savior and Lord (John 1:12).
2. That I have been baptized as a believer in Jesus Christ, and am an active member of this church (Acts 2:41-47).
3. That I believe the Bible to be the inspired Word of God (2 Peter 1:20-21).
4. That I believe Christian workers should be an example

of the believer in word, in conversation, in charity, in spirit, in faith, in purity, giving attendance to reading, to exhortation, to doctrine (1 Timothy 4:12, 13).

5. That I believe God has called me to serve Him and that this opportunity comes from Him.
6. That I believe the doctrines of this church and will adhere to its doctrinal statement.

FURTHERMORE, I WILL ENDEAVOR TO BE FAITHFUL IN THE FOLLOWING AREAS:

1. I will regularly attend the Sunday school, Sunday morning and evening services, the midweek services, and the soul-winning and visitation programs of the church (Hebrews 10:24-25).
2. I will regularly attend the workers' meetings.
3. I will visit prospects and visitors for the church, and do my best to be a personal soul-winner.
4. I will adhere to the church's policy concerning separation from the world on such matters as drinking, smoking, dancing, movies, and immodest dress (Colossians 3:17).
5. I will cooperate with my fellow workers, serving for the greatest good of the church (Ephesians 4:1-3).
6. I will be an example unto fellow members by giving at least one-tenth of my income to support this local church (Malachi 3:10).
7. I will be loyal to the pastor and programs of this church.
8. If I should ever become unwilling or unable to meet these requirements, I will resign my position rather than bring a reproach upon the church.[13]

Signed:_____
(Worker)

Some churches have a nominating committee which works with the pastor to make nominations of church officers. Then the church approves these nominations. Church officers should be elected by the church in this way, but many churches are finding that Sunday school teachers and Church Training leaders can be better chosen by the pastor and a Christian education committee. These teachers and workers appointed serve indefinitely, as long as they fulfill the responsibilities of their positions. Theirs is much like the indefinite call of a pastor. This allows for individual recruitment which is a better way of securing workers.[14]

Keeping Workers

Once the worker has been recruited he needs a job description. Much frustration among church workers can occur because no one has explained what their responsibilities will be. Many become defeated and resign their positions because they do not know what to do. So, a job description is very important.

After thoroughly understanding what their duties are, workers then need to be trained. One of the first things a new church needs is a teacher training course to equip teachers to do an effective job in the classroom. Ushers should be trained in greeting and seating visitors, getting visitors cards, and receiving the offering. Deacons should be trained in their responsibilities. Counselors need training in how to deal with those responding to the invitations. These workers need to be trained thoroughly and carefully, as eternal souls are at stake.[15] The problem of the shortage of teachers, personal workers, and soul-winners can best be solved by an effective training program.

Workers need to be motivated and encouraged. A weekly meeting is important to solve difficulties and motivate the workers. Special events and campaigns can be explained and excitement generated. The chief motive that causes most people to serve is love. Love for Christ, the church, and the pastor will get the work done by laymen who are thus motivated.

There are many ways to let workers know they are appreciated. They should be complimented personally for their faithfulness. They should be commended publicly on occasion. On Sunday night, a group of people who have worked hard could be honored. They could be mentioned in the church paper. The pastor could write notes of commendation to deserving workers.[16]

If the pastor loves his people and desires to help them accomplish the task God has given them, he will find ways to commend and encourage them to keep them on the firing line for God. An installation service should be held each year for all workers, and faithfulness rewarded throughout the year.

Accountability of Workers

The General Motors Corporation says, "People do not do what is expected. They do what is inspected." When a worker has been recruited and trained he should be left free to do his job, but his work should be checked.[17] The worker should be given a job description by the pastor, with a clear-cut understanding that involves no overlapping area of responsibility and no area left out. The pastor should have a weekly conference with each worker or a weekly workers' meeting to check up on progress in varied areas of responsibility and give assistance and direction to the future.

Workers should be directly responsible to their immediate supervisor. Teachers are responsible to department superintendents, and department superintendents are responsible to the general superintendent. However, all workers and staff members are directly or indirectly responsible to the pastor.

The pastor should receive copies of all reports at the weekly workers' conference so that he can know what each worker is doing.[18] He should be very observant about how the work is being done. Regularly scheduled planning meetings are essential to coordinate the work of the staff, church officers, and other workers. A well informed worker is a happy worker. Clearly defined areas of responsibility and authority frequently communicated can produce a smooth and productive staff relationship.

When a worker becomes a bad testimony to the church, he should be replaced. The pastor should never enjoy replacing a worker, but should do it with a broken heart. No worker should be replaced until he has been counseled. It should be explained exactly what he has done that disqualifies him to serve. He should understand that his consecration, not his resignation, is desired. If the worker will rededicate his life and again meet the requirements for workers, he should remain in his position. If he cannot or will not meet the requirements, he should be asked to resign. The pastor should deal immediately with workers who need to be replaced.[19]

Sometimes workers need to be reprimanded. The pastor should always do this privately and in love, not scolding, but showing them where they are wrong and how to correct the problem.[20]

The Staff

Church workers are divided into three groups—volunteer workers, part-time paid workers, and full-time paid staff. The mission church should become self-supporting before paid staff members are added. However, many times dedicated and talented laymen can assume responsibilities in specialized areas on a voluntary basis or for small part-time salaries. This can result in greater productivity with less total spending. Then as the church grows other staff members can be added.

The first staff member that needs to be employed is a church secretary. This person can be a real asset and should be secured by a new church as quickly as possible. Because she must work closely with the pastor, it is necessary that she be a person who is above question in morals, modest in dress, enthusiastic about her job, and loyal to the pastor. The secretary should be a lady whom the pastor's wife endorses. She must have an unreproachable reputation. A secretary can be a great asset to the pastor or a great detriment. She must be capable of keeping confidential things confidential.[21]

The following is a list of things the secretary can do for the pastor and church.

1. Answer the telephone and keep a record of all calls.
2. Type the pastor's letters and proofread his work.
3. Type the follow-up and promotional letters.
4. Sign form letters for the pastor.
5. Take telephone calls for the pastor, but be very careful not to speak for him in transmitting the message.
6. Make appointments for the pastor, keeping a copy of the church calendar and the pastor's personal calendar.

7. Give the pastor reminders of appointments and schedules.
8. Greet people for the pastor and the church.
9. Get flight reservations and information.
10. Type pulpit announcements, church bulletins, and order of service cards.
11. Be the custodian of the pastor's office.
12. File the pastor's sermons, lessons, and Bible studies.
13. Mimeograph forms and materials for the church.
14. Order office supplies, church supplies, and promotional items.
15. Send bulk mailings such as midweek papers, promotional leaflets, and appeal letters.[22]

The church should add staff members when the need arises. The growth of the church will come to a standstill unless additional staff members are hired. After a church secretary is secured, additional staff members may include associate pastor, bus director, director of Christian education, youth minister, music minister, visitation director, financial secretary, custodians, day-care and Christian school personnel.[23]

Approximately one new staff member is needed for each one hundred new people attending the church. There are approximately twenty giving units per one hundred persons. A person who holds down a job and pays his tithes is a giving unit. Ten new giving units provide enough money to support an additional staff member.[24]

Even though the church appropriates the necessary funds for needed staff members, they should work solely for the pastor.[25] It is impossible for a staff member to take orders from many different church members. To have a dozen different church members giving job descriptions and duties to a staff member will result in confusion and frustration. Therefore, the pastor must act as the coordinator between the church and staff. He should be responsible for hiring and dismissing staff members, with his decisions being ratified by the church. Blessed is the fortunate pastor who has a wonderful cooperative staff to assist him in the work of winning the lost to Christ and building up the saints in the faith.

The Deacons

Even though the duties and qualifications of deacons have already been discussed in the chapter on the church constitution and bylaws, further examination needs to be made of these important offices. The new church should not be too hasty in selecting deacons. These should be mature men who have proven their love for Christ and dedication to the church. Too often someone has been ordained as a deacon during a peak time of his Christian experience, and the church is plagued with a man who is unqualified.

It is important to hold as closely as possible to the standards for deacons as outlined in the Scriptures. It might be better to appoint an advisory committee until such time as God gives the church some men who meet the qualifications.[26]

Deacons should be separated from the world, agree with the doctrines, practices, and convictions of the church, be faithful to the services, be soul-winners, and be loyal to the pastor.[27] The deacons are to be servants in temporal matters and helpers to the pastor. The church in Jerusalem chose seven deacons to minister food to the widows in order to free the apostles so they could give themselves to prayer and to the ministry of the Word.

The responsibilities of deacons are soul-winning, doing personal work at the altar, assisting the pastor during the ordinances, assisting the pastor with church discipline, and visiting the sick and shut-ins.[28] They are members of the advisory board. They assist in drawing up the church budget, help count the offerings, make recommendations to the advisory board, assist with baptisms, the Lord's supper, and the feet washing services.[29]

A deacon should be chosen with extreme care and Scriptural standards should be strictly observed. The man should have the total approval of the pastor and all existing deacons before being considered. The pastor should meet with the man, explain carefully the qualifications, responsibilities, duties, and honor of being a deacon.[30] The man should have time to pray about his answer. If his answer is yes, the church then votes to put him on trial for a year. After the end of that year, and the vote of approval of the church, he is ordained for life or the maintenance of Christian character, but holds office at the pleasure of the church. He serves for a term of two years and may be reelected.

Conclusion

Behind every effective pastor is the power and strength of a slate of officers, teachers, and staff members. Behind every effective, growing church are the power and strength of a pastor and slate of workers who work together in providing the motivating force for the entire congregation.[31]

It is impossible for a group of men and women bound together in common spirit and understanding, united around a common cause, to fail to enjoy the blessings of God upon their combined efforts. If the pastor will honor his workers, love and encourage them, they will be the best friends he ever had, and will make him successful in building a great church for God.[32]

Chapter VIII
Reference Notes

[1]Elmer Towns, *Getting a Church Started in the Face of Insurmountable Odds with Limited Resources in Unlikely Circumstances* (Nashville: Impact Books, 1975), p. 157.

[2]Charles M. Underwood, editor, *Planting the Independent Fundamental Church* (Greenville, South Carolina: Bob Jones University, 1972), p. 65.

[3]Wayne C. Clark, *The Minister Looks at Himself* (Chicago: The Judson Press, 1957), p. 15.

[4]Melvin L. Hodges, *A Guide to Church Planting* (Chicago: Moody Press, 1973), p. 76. Used by permission.

[5]Jim McAllister, "Points for Preachers," *The Gem* (January, 1977), p. 10.

[6]Howard F. Snyden and Warren W. Wiersbe, *When the Pastor Wonders How* (Chicago: Moody Press, 1973), p. 82. Used by permission.

[7]Towns, p. 85.

[8]Underwood, pp. 65-66.

[9]Jack Hyles, *The Hyles Church Manual* (Murfreesboro, Tennessee: Sword of the Lord Publishers, 1968), p. 272.

[10]Lee Lebsack, *Ten at the Top* (Stow, Ohio: New Hope

Press, 1974), p. 15.

11 Snyden and Wiersbe, p. 83.

12 Underwood, p. 65.

13 Dale Burden, *Workers' Covenant* (Norfolk, Virginia: Fairmount Park Free Will Baptist Church, n.d.), p. 1.

14 Curtis Hutson, *Pastors' and Workers' Conference* (Decatur, Georgia: Forrest Hills Baptist Church, n.d.), p. 3.

15 Hodges, p. 43.

16 Hyles, p. 273.

17 Don Wardell, *Practical Help for Christian Workers* (Winona Lake, Indiana: Wardell Publishers, 1974), p. 82.

18 Lebsack, p. 16.

19 Hutson, p. 5.

20 *Ibid.*, p. 6.

21 Underwood, pp. 22-23.

22 Hyles, p. 275.

23 Lebsack, p. 15.

24 Jerry Falwell and Elmer Towns, *Church Aflame* (Nashville: Impact Books, 1971), p. 185.

25 *Ibid.*, p. 188.

26 Hodges, p. 53..

27 Hyles, p. 72.

28 George Godfrey, *Helps to Have a Soul Winning Church* (Crown Point, Indiana: Hyles-Anderson College, 1976), p. 20.

29 Hyles, p. 74.

30 *Ibid.*, p. 70.

31 Leslie Parrot, *Building Today's Church* (Grand Rapids: Baker Book House, 1973), p. 49.

32 John Bisagno, *How to Build an Evangelistic Church* (Nashville: Broadman Press, 1972), p. 49. Used by permission.

CHAPTER IX

THE SUNDAY SCHOOL

The Sunday school is the church at work, reaching, teaching, winning the lost, then training them for Christian service.[1] This means that the primary purpose for the Sunday school is not Bible teaching, but evangelism.[2] This is not to say that the Sunday school is not to teach the Bible. The Bible is the textbook of the Sunday school. But the primary purpose of the Sunday school is evangelism. More people are brought to Christ and into the church through the Sunday school than any other way.

The Sunday school has seven definite purposes. First, it is to win the lost to Christ. Second, those won are to be baptized. Third, saved people are to be enlisted for church membership. Fourth, the Word of God is to be taught. Fifth, people are to learn the grace of giving. Sixth, people are to be taught how to serve Christ. Seventh, converts are to be trained to win others.[3] The pastor will do well to build a good Sunday school, because the major growth of the church will come through it.

Organization

Proper organization is essential to a thriving Sunday school. Too much organization can add weights, and too little organization can prevent its operating with peak efficiency.

Some Sunday schools choose to operate under a separate constitution and bylaws. A sample constitution for a Free Will Baptist Sunday school can be obtained from the Sunday School and Church Training Department, P.O. Box 17306, Nashville, Tennessee 37217. The Sunday school should remember that it is the church at study and at work. It should never divorce itself from the work of the church, and the church and its officers should never separate themselves from the Sunday school.[4]

As the leader of the church, the pastor is overseer of the Sunday school. He should, by all means, attend Sunday school and take an active part. He should definitely be the leader whether behind the scenes or before the people. The pastor is the one to initiate a teacher training program. He should conduct the officers' and teachers' meetings, plan the promotional activities, and give leadership and encouragement throughout the entire Sunday school program.[5]

There are many advantages to the pastor teaching a class. It should be an adult class, perhaps an auditorium Bible class. The pastor is the best teacher in the church, because he has the most preparation and experience in teaching. He knows more about the Bible. He will be able to draw more people into his class than any other person because of his background, position, and respect. He will have more time to spend in visitation to build the class. It is the opinion of the author that the pastor should teach an adult class, especially in the beginning.

As the church grows, the pastor can start other classes from his class. This is another reason the pastor should teach. He will be willing to lose the pupils and teachers to form other classes, while another teacher might not.

Large, growing, soul-winning Sunday schools are always the result of planning, praying, and hard work. The pastor who wants a successful Sunday school must be a prominent figure in Sunday school leadership.[6]

The board or committee of Christian education is elected

by the church to work with the pastor in overseeing the work of Christian education in the local church. The reasons for establishing a Christian education committee might be summed up in one word—success.[7]

The membership of this committee is composed of the pastor who is an ex officio member of all boards and committees, the general Sunday school superintendent who is the chairman, the Church Training Director, and as many other members as the church may choose. The members should be mature Christians who have training or experience in Christian education.[8]

The purpose of the Christian education committee is to coordinate the educational work of the church to achieve peak efficiency. It assists the pastor, superintendent, and staff in their heavy responsibilities, and gives teachers and workers support. It works with the pastor in providing for a training program, and facilitates action in the educational work of the church.[9]

It is the responsibility of this committee to plan and maintain a comprehensive program of Christian education. It establishes all policies for the educational programs of the church with respect to materials, personnel, meeting times, and meeting places of classes and groups within the church.

This committee selects and approves all educational literature and supplies. It outlines teaching methods along with goals and objectives. It selects, trains, and approves leaders and teaching staff. Planning for future needs is a part of the responsibility of the Christian education committee.[10]

This committee, working with the pastor, will place all workers in the Sunday school and CTS, so committee members should be chosen with care. They should be members of the church who realize the important function of this committee. Next in line in Sunday school organization is the general superintendent. The church should elect the man for this position who knows the most about Sunday school and is the best leader in the Sunday school. He is often considered second in importance to the pastor. Until a man with vision, dedication, burden, and understanding comes along to fill this position, the pastor may want to serve as Sunday school superintendent.[11]

The Sunday school superintendent is a spiritual pacesetter. He should have distinguished himself as one who is faithful to church and loyal to the pastor. He administrates the Sunday school by directing its workers and serving as chairman of the Christian education committee.[12]

He should not consume the teachers' time on Sunday morning with a long devotion or a drawn out opening exercise. He is to give supervision to the entire program of the Sunday school and see that it runs smoothly and efficiently.[13]

He should oversee the work of the Sunday school along with the pastor. He should be the dynamic inspiration behind the enlistment of workers, the choosing of the departmental superintendents, the keeping of the records, and every other phase of the Sunday school program.[14]

The department superintendents work directly under the general Sunday school superintendent. They are the key people as far as promoting attendance is concerned. They are responsible for directing the work of their respective departments. Their main duty is to keep the departments running smoothly and inspire and challenge the workers.

The department superintendents conduct the opening assembly for the departments, fill any vacancies when teachers are absent, and oversee the work of the departments. The most important of their responsibilities is promoting attendance. When an attendance campaign is in progress, the department superintendents are key people who motivate the workers to make the departments grow.[15]

The pastor should aim at the goal of having a department for every age group. That would be a cradle roll department, a nursery department, a beginner department, a primary department, a junior department, a junior high department, a senior high department, a young adult department, and an adult department.[16] But the church does not want to start with all of these. The Sunday school should not departmentalize until it has the number and workers to enable it to do so.

When the Sunday school is departmentalized, three departments should be sufficient at first. A children's department could include cradle roll through juniors. A youth department could be composed of a junior high through high school. An adult department could be those from young adulthood through senior citizens.[17] Other departments could be added as the need arises. Too many departments organized before the church is ready will result in unqualified workers being used.[18]

The teachers are very important people because they teach the Word of God to the pupils, lead them to Christ, and visit in their homes. Just as the pastor takes spiritual oversight of the entire church, the Sunday school teacher takes spiritual oversight of the class. The teachers are to uphold the doctrines and standards of the church both by teaching and daily living. They should qualify themselves through the teacher training programs of the church and take advantage of every opportunity to grow to be better teachers.

They are to attend all services of the church, tithe, live

clean lives, prepare the lesson faithfully, visit the absentees and prospects, work to build the class, and love the pupils. Teachers should contact the department superintendents as soon as they learn they will be unable to be present for Sunday school.

Teachers in training can be used effectively to develop new teachers for the Sunday school. These workers can go into the classrooms with the teachers while they are training to become teachers. They can serve as the class secretaries, assist the teachers, and learn from them. They can teach when the teachers have to be absent. When the classes grow large enough to split, the teachers in training can take part of the pupils and form new classes.

The teacher and class secretary should be present to greet pupils when they enter the classroom. If envelopes or record slips are used, these should be distributed. The secretary should be sure that each visitor has a visitor's card, and then make sure the card is filled out and returned. The class secretary should take the roll, record the absentees, count the offering, and deposit these items in the proper place for the department secretary.[19]

Care should be taken that reports are filled out as soon as possible so that department secretaries can get the results to the general secretary. The class secretary should be a responsible person who will see that records are accurately kept, and that the teacher receives a list of all visitors and absentees.

The following is a checklist which can be used for a teacher or a teacher in training.

1. Do I live a separated life?
2. Do I have a daily private devotion?
3. Is my thought life pure?

4. Do I start studying my lesson on Monday, reviewing it throughout the week?
5. Do I have the right motives, such as love for my pupils?
6. Am I prepared physically, mentally, and spiritually to teach?
7. Do I pray daily for each pupil?
8. Do I visit all of my absentees weekly?
9. Have I visited in the home of each pupil this quarter?
10. Am I a pastor to my pupils?
11. Do I attend teachers' meetings?
12. Do I support the entire church program?
13. Am I loyal to my pastor?
14. When I am absent, do I contact my superintendent early?
15. Do I get up early enough on Sunday morning?
16. Do I review my lesson again on Sunday morning?
17. Do I arrive at least fifteen minutes before Sunday school begins?
18. Do I make my classroom attractive?
19. Do I greet my class members as they arrive?
20. Do I meet any visitors before class?
21. Are my visitors properly introduced in class?
22. Do I enlist any new members?
23. Does my class spend a maximum of five minutes on preliminaries?
24. Do I get all visitors to properly fill out visitor's cards?
25. Do I remember not to make any pupil read or talk unless voluntarily?
26. Do I have an interest getter for my lesson?
27. Do I stay on the subject?
28. Do I seek to win my pupils to Christ by giving an

invitation in class when necessary?
29. Do I sit with lost pupils during the worship service?
30. Do I do everything possible during the week to win
lost pupils to Christ?[20]

The general Sunday school secretary is also an important office in the Sunday school. Her job is to tabulate all the statistics from the departments so that the results of the work of each Sunday may be known. She gives the total attendance, offering, visitors present, and other important information to the general superintendent and the pastor.

Some Sunday schools like to organize individual classes with class officers. This can be done if desired.[21]

If the pastor will see that his Sunday school is organized properly and staffed with qualified workers, it will keep his church constantly growing. In fact, most church growth will come through the Sunday school.

Teacher Training

The church planter should begin immediately a program of teacher training. In the outset, a "crash course" will need to be used to give beginning teachers a plan to follow in doing the work. The National Home Missions Department has a booklet which may be used to meet this immediate need. It is titled *The Sunday School Teacher's Guide.*

The pastor should begin immediately to enroll people in an extensive teacher training course. Some of the best are the courses published by the Evangelical Teacher Training Association. Two vital and challenging courses of study are available, one preliminary and the other advanced. Each course consists of three courses in Bible and three in Christian education. If the courses are taught by a teacher who has earned the ETTA Teacher's diploma, and the students meet necessary requirements, three semester hours credit will be allowed by Free Will Baptist Bible College, Nashville, Tennessee, for both the preliminary and the advanced courses.[22]

The Free Will Baptist Sunday School and Church Training Department also has a teacher training course written by Free Will Baptist writers. A certificate is issued when each book is completed, and then a diploma is granted upon completion of the entire course.

A teacher training class could be conducted on Sunday nights, on Wednesday nights, during the Church Training hour, or any time at the pastor's discretion. A teacher training program is so very important in the building of a strong church. A perpetual teacher training class should be conducted by the church which continually turns out graduates and enrolls new teachers in training.

Teachers and workers should also be encouraged to become students of the Word of God and do everything they can to prepare themselves for their important tasks. They should be encouraged to attend available workshops, seminars, and conferences on Sunday school and church growth methods. They should constantly be exposed to new teaching techniques, new materials and equipment, and new ways to convey God's Word to the lost.

Officers' and Teachers' Meeting

The next thing the pastor should do is begin a weekly

officers' and teachers' meeting. Some churches have a monthly officers' and teachers' meeting, while others just meet spasmodically. However, in the beginning of a new church, a weekly officers' and teachers' meeting is needed.

Such a meeting will promote teamwork among the workers and pastor. In these meetings the plans for the following Sunday are made. Teachers receive inspiration, and methods and techniques for teaching the lesson for the coming Sunday are given. Excitement is generated for promotions being used, and workers are challenged to reach attendance goals.

This meeting is really a "pep rally" where the pastor recognizes those who have done good jobs, and inspires those who have not. It offers a time for Christian fellowship, which is desperately needed in a new church. It also insures a good crowd, if it is conducted on the same night as the midweek service.[23]

The following is a suggested outline for the weekly officers' and teachers' meeting.

Provide a meal at the church for the workers getting off late from work. Have those who can bring a vegetable dish or salad. The church could provide the meat. Set the time at 6:00 P.M. and eat together. An offering may be taken at the end of the meal which would take care of the expense of the meat.

From 6:30 to 6:50 is a period of inspiration and promotion. Last Sunday's attendance is discussed and the workers are challenged about goals and promotional ideas for the next Sunday.

From 6:50 to 7:10 the pastor should go over the lesson with the teachers. This will greatly help them do an effective job and will enable the pastor to give them proper interpretation of the Scriptures and things he wants emphasized.

From 7:10 to 7:25 the application is given to the lesson. If the Sunday school is departmentalized, each department should meet together. There each department superintendent should explain the visual aids, object lessons, and other things that can be used to drive the lesson into the hearts of the pupils. Until the Sunday school departmentalizes, the pastor can break the lesson down to various age levels, introducing related object lessons and illustrations.

The meeting should conclude promptly at 7:25 so that the midweek service can start promptly at 7:30. The pastor should strive to see that this time schedule is followed closely.[24]

Through such a meeting the pastor will gather about him a corps of workers, build them up in the faith, and send them forth to reach the city for Christ. The officers' and teachers' meeting is necessary in any Sunday school that wants an efficient, trained, and qualified staff.

Follow-Up of Absentees and Prospects

Teachers best show their interest and concern when they visit in the homes of their pupils. Every pupil should be visited at least once each quarter. There is no substitute for a home visit to help the teacher become acquainted with the background, interests, and problems of those in the classroom. There cannot be an effective teaching ministry until something is known of the spiritual condition and needs of the individual.

The teacher should receive a list of visitors and absentees each week from the Sunday school secretary or class secretary. Every absentee and visitor should be contacted before the following Sunday.

In case of absence, a telephone call is sufficient for the first Sunday in many cases. The second Sunday, the teacher should visit in the home without fail and try to get the pupil back to Sunday school. The third Sunday, the department superintendent should call on the absentee. After he has been absent four Sundays, the general superintendent or the pastor should visit the absentee and try to secure his return to Sunday school.[25]

Pupils should not be dropped from the roll unless they move away or join another Sunday school. As long as they are listed on the class rolls, they should be worked with, prayed for, and every effort should be made to win them to Christ and build them up in the faith.

Literature and Supplies

The use of Sunday school literature was discontinued by a number of churches a few years ago. However, many are returning to the use of literature. They found that Sunday school is the one agency in the church that can give a systematic, comprehensive, complete coverage of Scripture and doctrine. When a local church does not have a systematic curriculum, it usually goes off on tangents, omits important doctrines, or overemphasizes the preacher's "pet hobby horse."

In a new work, where the church is not established in the city, it is worth much to have an attractive quarterly to place in the hands of new people. If quarterlies have our name on them, this will show visitors to the new church that is is not alone in its endeavor.

Sunday school literature gives the pastor more time for visitation and the many other tasks necessary to planting and growing a church. His time will not have to be taken up writing and printing Sunday school literature, which can be an expensive undertaking, especially for a new church with a beginning budget. Literature gives pupils the opportunity to study the lesson beforehand and provides daily Bible readings.

Free Will Baptists have some of the finest Sunday school literature available anywhere, written and published by our own Sunday School Department. It takes the adult students through the Bible in seven years, and the children in three and two year cycles. Special days such as Christmas and Easter are remembered in the lesson plans. Family devotions can be planned around the daily Bible readings, which encourages family study of the Bible. New churches will do well to avail themselves of these materials.

The Free Will Baptist Sunday School and Church Training Department also publishes a complete system of Sunday school record keeping supplies. There are enrollment cards for each member of the Sunday school. Attendance slips and offering envelopes are printed for pupils to check attendance each Sunday. Class record books, departmental record books, and general Sunday school record books are provided so that accurate records can be kept throughout the Sunday school. The general record is in triplicate so the superintendent and pastor can both receive a copy, with one copy remaining in the book for a permanent record.

Visitors' cards are printed along with visitation assignment cards. A complete catalog is provided by the Sunday School Department of other available supplies, but the above mentioned will be needed to begin and conduct the Sunday school.

In a new church, the pastor may need to improvise as far as providing Sunday school classrooms for each class. The building and rooms may be far from desirable. However, even from the beginning, a new church can use excellent equipment. Chalkboards and flannelgraph boards in good condition will be needed throughout the Sunday school. A good set of Bible maps is very helpful. Overhead projectors, and slide and filmstrip projectors can also be used effectively.

Puppets are some of the most popular tools used in teaching children today. Television has taught the church that these things can be very effective in the teaching process.

A church library needs to be started as soon as possible to give a frame of reference to the people of the church for their study. If operated properly a church library can also be a source of inspiration as well as instruction if new books are constantly added.

Sunday school literature, record supplies, visual aid equipment, and object lessons are all tools a church must use if it is to effectively teach God's Word. A new church will be wise to invest in securing these if it wants to have a growing, effective Sunday school that is meeting the needs of people.

Attendance Campaigns

In order to build a great Sunday school much attention must be given to promotion. Contests, enlargement campaigns, and special days do ten things for a Sunday school.

1. They unify the church.
2. They attract crowds.
3. They cause church members to work.

4. They stimulate teachers.
5. They emphasize evangelism.
6. They reach the community.
7. They encourage visitation.
8. They excite the entire church.
9. They boost attendance permanently.
10. They cause church building and expansion.[26]

The Free Will Baptist Sunday School and Church Training Department sponsors a spring and fall enlargement campaign each year. They publish all the materials for planning, promoting, and conducting the entire campaign. Churches which enter are placed in a division according to their size so they are competing with other Free Will Baptist churches across the country. At the end of the campaign, results are tabulated and the winners' names published and trophies awarded.

Attack, a reach out enrollment plan for Sunday schools, is also printed by the Free Will Baptist Sunday School and Church Training Department. Churches that have used this plan have experienced increases in Sunday school attendance in excess of forty percent.[27]

With a little imagination, all kinds of special days could be arranged. The following are some of those big days:

1. Once each year a *Back to School Sunday* could be conducted, awarding each school child with a gift.
2. *Teacher Appreciation Sunday* may be promoted by having each pupil try to give his teacher the biggest class ever on that day.
3. *Carry the Load Sunday* asks each department to work hard for one week. Each week a different department

would "carry the load."

4. *Baseball Sunday* carries the baseball theme throughout the Sunday school with team competition between classes.

5. *Round Up Sunday* could come at the end of vacations when all the "strays" are rounded up.

6. *Homecoming Day* is conducted in many churches to commemorate the birthday of the founding of the church.

7. *Broken Heart Sunday* is a good emphasis around Valentine's Day to bring back absentees.

8. *Bible Conference Day* could award those bringing a certain number of visitors a trip to the Bible conference at one of the Free Will Baptist colleges.

9. *Vacation Bible School Sunday* is conducted on the Sunday climaxing the Vacation Bible School.

10. *Old Fashioned Day* is one of the best special days. Old fashioned clothes, singing, preaching, and "dinner on the ground" can be emphasized.

11. *Record Breaking Day* can be used to great advantages almost anywhere to break all previous attendance records.

12. *Patriotic Sunday* is good for the 4th of July weekend.[28]

Other suggestions for big days are Baby Day, Picture Taking Day, Good Neighbor Sunday, B-1 Sunday, Easter Sunday, Christmas Sunday, Bus Sunday, Youth Day, Mission Impossible Sunday, Mother's Day, Father's Day, Senior Citizen's Sunday, Armed Forces Sunday, and Missions Sunday. There is no end to special days that can be observed and contests that the Lord can use to help excite the people and build attendance.

Conclusion

Once the Sunday school is organized and functioning properly, the pastor will need to constantly watch and study it to keep it moving. When a class or department ceases to grow, he should discover the problem area and work to solve it. The Free Will Baptist Sunday School Department has a standard of achievement by which to gauge the progress. These should be obtained and displayed throughout the classrooms.

The pastor will need to reorganize, split classes, and begin departments as the work grows. He should constantly be watching for new workers to fit into the Sunday school, because as workers are added, the Sunday school will grow. Through proper planning and hard work any new church can develop a Sunday school that is reaching the lost and teaching the saved.

Chapter IX
Reference Notes

[1]Elmer Towns, *The Successful Sunday School and Teacher's Guidebook* (Carol Stream, Illinois: Creation House, 1976), p. 19. Used by permission.

[2]Lee Lebsack, *Ten at the Top* (Stow, Ohio: New Hope Press, 1974), p. 16.

[3]Curtis Hutson, *Pastor's and Workers'* Conference (Decatur, Georgia: Forrest Hills Baptist Church, n.d.), p. 2.

[4]Jack Hyles, *The Hyles Sunday School Manual* (Murfreesboro, Tennessee: Sword of the Lord Publishers, 1969), p. 9.

[5]Hyles, p. 10.

[6]Tom Malone, *The Sunday School Reaching Multitudes* (Murfreesboro, Tennessee: Sword of the Lord Publishers, 1973), p. 38.

[7]Towns, p. 72.

[8]Clate A. Risley and W. Donald Reeder, editors, *The Sunday School Encyclopedia*, XI (Chicago: National Sunday School Association, 1962), p. 26.

[9]*Ibid.*

[10]Towns, pp. 75-77.

[11]*Ibid.*, p. 83.

[12]George S. McNeill, editor, *The Sunday School Encyclopedia*, XII (Wheaton, Illinois: National Sunday School Association, 1965), p. 67.

[13]Risley, p. 29.

[14]Hyles, p. 10.

[15]*Ibid.*

[16]Risley, p. 31.

[17]McNeill, p. 68.

[18]Hyles, p. 11.

[19]*Ibid.*, p. 18.

[20]Robert Shockey, *The Sunday School Teacher's Guide* (Nashville: Free Will Baptist Board of Home Missions, 1975), p. 6.

[21]*Ibid.*

[22]Harrold D. Harrison, *Commissioned to Communicate* (Nashville: Free Will Baptist Sunday School Department, 1969), p. 1.

[23]Malone, pp. 100-102.

[24]Hyles, pp. 99-111.

[25]Towns, pp. 225-227.

[26]*Ibid.*, p. 231.

[27]Roger C. Reeds, editor, *Attack* (Nashville: Randall House Publications, 1977), p. 5.

[28]Hyles, pp. 130-154.

CHAPTER X

SOUL-WINNING, VISITATION, AND FOLLOW-UP

The purpose of building a new congregation must be to win people to Christ. Without soul-winning as the single purpose for its existence, a new congregation is miscarried before its birth, or will languish in the dull stupor of feeble religious routine. The church of Jesus Christ was conceived in love and given life through the birth pangs of Calvary. To conceive a new congregation outside the bounds of love for sinners is to bring forth an illegitimate imposter.[1]

The pastor is the key to the evangelistic work of the church. If the pastor is evangelistic, others will follow his example. If the pastor is cold and dead about soul-winning, he can be absolutely sure that the rest of the church will not get on fire to reach others for Christ. Thus, the pastor must do the work of an evangelist. He leads the church in this most important work.[2]

House-to-house, door-to-door visitation is God's plan in action. Going from one home to another, street by street, block by block, is the most methodical means to present Jesus to every individual. In Acts 2:46-47 it is not impossible to assume that these early Christians made it their purpose to visit every home in Jerusalem so that they could present Christ to each resident. Door-to-door visitation is the most effective and methodical means to tell the gospel to every creature. The early church multiplied their number by visiting house-to-house in personal soul-winning. It will work today wherever this example is followed.

House-to-house visitation is where the material is gathered

to build a new congregation. It is the heart of the Great Commission. The church planter will be wise to destroy every discouragement, excuse, or activity that would keep him from going where the unsaved are found. A new congregation cannot be built without house-to-house visitation.[3]

The *Attack* program of the Free Will Baptist Sunday School Department is excellent to put the whole church out knocking doors, going house-to-house, street by street. The National Home Missions Department has door-to-door survey sheets and telephone survey information which can be used. These are tools which will aid the members of the new congregation to become personal soul-winners.

The pastor will begin his church with a month of door knocking in preparation for his "get acquainted" services. Even after the church has been organized, he should never get so busy that he does not have at least one afternoon a week to get out and knock on new doors.

Where to Get Prospects

The success of any visitation program depends on getting good prospects. The following methods of locating the unchurched are being used by some growing churches in various parts of the nation.

1. Distribute the cards to everyone at the church services and request them to list any unchurched families they know. There will be some people in the Sunday morning service who are not in Sunday school, and this reminds all members to be on the watch for prospects constantly.

2. Some of the best prospects a church will have are the people who visit its services. In order to follow up on these

people, their names and addresses must be obtained. The best way to get the information needed is by the use of visitors' cards. The following is a step-by-step procedure to be followed in getting these cards filled out. The ushers will need a good supply of visitors' cards and pencils, and be trained in proper procedures of distribution.

a. The pastor welcomes the visitors. This welcome should be warm, friendly, sincere, and with good eye contact.

b. When the pastor begins to welcome the visitors, the ushers (who have been standing in the rear of the church) walk down the aisles to the front. (There should be one in each side aisle and two in the main aisles.) If the auditorium is large, one set of ushers should stand at the front of the building, and a second set of ushers should be positioned in the middle of the building.

c. When the ushers reach their positions they should turn and *face the audience.*

d. At the proper place in his welcome the pastor will say, "Will every person with us for the first time today raise your hand *with me?*" As he raises his hand the visitors will raise theirs.

e. As soon as the hands are raised the ushers give each visitor a visitors' card and a pencil. (The ushers are already positioned so they can easily see the people.)

f. The pastor will say, "Our ushers will give you a visitors' card and a pencil. Will you please fill out the card and drop it in the offering plate when it is passed, and keep the pencil as a gift from our church?"

g. The ushers will get the visitors' cards from the offering plates and give them to the pastor.

h. All visitors should be contacted before the next Sunday.

i. File all the visitors' cards, but designate those who are prospects from those who are not.

j. Get visitors' cards in every service where visitors are present, such as regular Sunday services, midweek services, missionary conferences, Vacation Bible School commencement exercises, and revival services.[4]

3. Usually there are unchurched children and their parents among those who attend the Vacation Bible School. Visitors' cards should be filled out on these, and an appropriate letter and/or telephone call should be made.

4. Someone can examine all visitors' cards for those who live in the area and who are unchurched. This should be done each Sunday night and special visitation assignments made to selected workers for prompt visitation. Then these names can be added to the files for different geographical areas.

5. The following are eighteen possibilities for names and addresses of newcomers to the community. The newcomers can then be contacted by mail and/or telephone to determine if they are prospects for the church.

a. Chamber of Commerce
b. City hall
c. Welcome Wagon organizations
d. Newcomer Service, Welcome Newcomer, Key to the City

e. The person who takes orders for water service
f. The man who connects water meters
g. The person who takes orders for gas service
h. The man who connects gas meters
i. The person who takes orders for electrical service
j. The man who connects electric meters
k. The person who takes orders for telephone service
l. The man who installs new telephones
m. Real estate salesmen
n. Moving companies
o. Mortgage companies and lending agencies
p. Apartment managers
q. Managers of trailer parks
r. Personnel managers of large companies

Sometimes arrangements can be made with the utility companies to provide the information on their new customers, but if the utility companies themselves cannot provide this information, then sometimes arrangements can be made with individual employees of the companies. Sometimes some of these persons are already members of the church and could easily be recruited for this informational service. Many times arrangements can be made with the persons involved in writing orders for new customers or those involved in making the installations. If such arrangements can be made, it usually requires a very careful, diplomatic, and personal approach.

Some special research will be required to learn all possible sources of information on newcomers. These sources will need to provide information that will be complete, timely, dependable, and reliable. This will often involve some cost, either per month or per family, but this is vital, valuable information a

church can obtain. It is a proven fact that some of the
newcomers will almost automatically join some church in the
area and others may be considered as evangelistic prospects.[5]

6. The colleges, universities, trade schools, and other
special training schools in the area should be considered as a
source of information. Many times information may be secured
on all new students at the beginning of each semester or
quarter. This information can sometimes be obtained from the
registrar or the dean of students.

7. When the new telephone directory is distributed each
year, canvass every family listed in the new telephone directory
that was not listed in the previous directory.

8. Distribute specially prepared leaflets or brochures to all
occupants of motels and hotels Saturday nights or early Sunday
mornings. Some churches even provide a copy of the Saturday
newspaper to all the occupants.

9. Mail specially prepared letters to names appearing in the
newspapers. This includes the newlyweds, the parents of
newborn babies, high school and college graduates, those
receiving promotions with employers, families involved in
tragedies (accidents, fires, thefts, drownings), the families of the
deceased in the obituary columns, and any other local names in
the news. Specially prepared letters can be printed that are
appropriate for each category. Postal cards can be enclosed for
the people to return to the church indicating one or more of the
following requests:

        a. For the pastor to visit
        b. For special prayer
        c. For a Bible
        d. For information about the church

e. For information about becoming a Christian

f. For their name to be added to the church mailing list

One or two people can be assigned to scan every newspaper in the area for names in the news. They can address envelopes, enclose the appropriate letters, church brochures, and the return postal cards. Then special attention can be given all cards returned to the church.

10. In the hospitals many times patients who are unchurched will be in rooms with church members. The pastor can meet them when visiting his members. Many times through special diplomatic efforts, the hospital will provide the pastor with names of patients who do not indicate any local church membership.

11. At the jails a pastor can usually visit the inmates and their families when visiting hours and facilities permit. Special letters can be sent appropriate to inmates' birthdays, trials, or releases.

12. New church members usually have acquaintances in the community who are unchurched. Each week someone can be assigned to telephone new families who joined the church the previous Sunday to ask for information on any unchurched family they know who might be prospects for the church.

13. Telephone answering machines and announcements in the personal columns of the newspapers appeal to those who are lonely, need advice, and are troubled. The church could purchase a telephone answering machine that will play a two minute message and then record the name and address of the caller after the message concludes.

14. Prospects can also be obtained from bus workers who will canvass the entire area covered by their bus routes. This can

result in many prospects of unchurched families and also prospects for bus riders.[6]

There are plenty of prospects and there are ways to obtain their names and addresses. The pastor who wants his church to grow will keep his visitation workers supplied with plenty of prospects.

Records and Supplies

Visitation is the most difficult service in the church to get people to attend. Therefore, it should be very well planned and promoted. There should be an up-to-date file on prospects with accurate records kept of visits made to the homes and the results of those visits. Prospect cards should be filled out in duplicate so that one will always remain in the permanent file. The pastor or visitation director should plan assignment cards in advance and have them ready when people arrive at the church to go out on visitation.

New Testaments should be on hand for any who may not have one. However, it is best to encourage people to use their own Bibles, marking the soul-winning Scriptures so they can find them more easily. New Testaments are also needed for the soul-winner to give to those he wins to Christ.

The pastor should keep plenty of good gospel tracts on hand for his people to leave in the homes where they visit. Everything distributed should have the church's name, address, telephone number, and the pastor's name on it.

The church should have brochures which give some information about the church, the time of services, the church program, and the plan of salvation. These should be supplied to all visitation workers in any type of church visitation or soul-winning program.

Some good maps of the city should be available to the visitation workers so they can find their prospects. These could be divided into geographical areas with teams sent to only one or two areas for their assignments. This will cut down on driving time and will result in more time for soul-winning.

Soul-winners should be encouraged to keep flashlights and telephone books in their cars. When visiting in areas where prospects live, they can look up the addresses.

Balloons and other items may be needed to give to children in homes where soul-winners are witnessing to parents. A soul-winning partner can keep children occupied with these items while the other is witnessing to the parents.

A supply of breath mints should also be kept at the church to be distributed to those going out on visitation.[7] Pencils should be supplied so teams can record the results of their visits on the assignment cards. All assignment cards should be returned to the church so results can be tabulated and recorded in the permanent prospect file.

Getting Lay People Involved

The task of visitation and soul-winning is so enormous the pastor cannot do it alone. He must train his people to do the work. In doing this he is doing the work of an evangelist, for he is extending his ministry in carrying the good news to those who are lost.[8]

The pastor begins getting his people involved by being a soul-winner and a faithful visitor himself. People will not work all week at a secular job and then go out to visit prospects unless they know the pastor is visiting all he can.

People will give priority to those things the pastor sees as important. Soul-winning and visitation activities should have top priority in the church. They should not be cancelled for any reason. The pastor should give a good part of his own time to soul-winning. If he has people coming down the aisle every week that he has won to Christ, it will encourage the people of the church to visit and win souls.

The pastor can also get lay people involved by magnifying soul-winners. The most important people are those who go with the gospel and bring in the lost. The leaders he appoints should be soul-winners. If a pastor places people in key positions who have no place in their lives for soul-winning and visitation, it will be difficult to get other people involved.

People must be taught how to witness and win souls if they are to get involved. One of the first things a church planter should do in beginning a new church is teach and preach on soul-winning.[9]

He should train others in how to win souls. A good dedicated man could be invited to go out with the pastor. Let him remain silent, but just go and listen and learn. Take him at least once a week for this "on the job training" for about three months or until he is able to go out with another soul-winning partner.[10] People can take classes on soul-winning for years, but they will never get the confidence to do it themselves until they are taken into people's homes for actual soul-winning experiences.[11]

Although the pastor should preach sermons on soul-winning, and teach classes on soul-winning, he must not "badger" the people about it, for this will cause them to rebel. Recruiting should be done, not only from the pulpit, but also on a person-to-person basis, first by the pastor and then by trained laymen.[12]

Sending people in pairs also helps get laymen involved. It is a Scriptural principle, for Jesus sent two to bring the borrowed colt in Luke 19:29, 30. He sent two to prepare the last supper in Luke 22:7, 8. Two heavenly messengers appeared on the Mount of Transfiguration in Luke 9:30. Two angels appeared at the ascension in Acts 1:10, 11. He sent the twelve in pairs in Matthew 10:1, 2, and the seventy two-by-two in Luke 10:1. Paul and Barnabas, Paul and Silas, and Barnabas and Mark are other pairs who were sent.

God blesses the two-by-two method because it assures the presence of Jesus (Matthew 18:20). He has promised to answer prayer when two pray (Matthew 18:19). The two-by-two method requires planning. It is a partnership method which enables each to draw strength and courage from the other. Going in pairs is the way of propriety. No tales of immorality, indecency, or impropriety will be told on those who go in pairs. People will go in pairs who will not go alone.[13]

An organized visitation program helps get people involved. Everyone needs a definite time to go.[14] If people are left to just go on their own time, many times they get busy and never take the time to go soul-winning. Setting a definite time helps people plan ahead for this service as they do any other church service.

Soul-winners can be recruited through a special banquet prepared for that purpose.[15] They can be challenged to sign faith promise soul-winning cards, committing themselves through God's help to try to win a given number of souls in a year's time.

Soul-winners should be honored when they win someone

to Christ. When the convert comes down the aisle to make public profession, the pastor should have the soul-winner come with him. The pastor should commend the soul-winner publicly and perhaps present him a fish hook lapel pin for being a "fisher of men."

If the pastor is a personal soul-winner himself, prays for his people to be soul-winners, preaches soul-winning in love, teaches soul-winning classes, provides plenty of prospects, sends each with a good partner, and provides soul-winning programs in which all his people can participate, he will have people involved in soul-winning and visitation. Getting lay people involved is absolutely necessary to have a growing, soul-winning church.

Visitation Programs

In order to get maximum participation and maximum results, there should be several kinds of visitation and soul-winning programs offered to the people.

The sick, shut-ins, and those in the hospital need to be visited. When people visit the services, the church should return that visit without fail the following week. Absentees from the Sunday school and delinquent church members must be visited. New converts and new church members need visits. Newcomers to the city can be visited. Families of bus children should be visited. Prospects gained in canvassing and other methods need visits. Then there is door-to-door visitation which needs to be done. Bus visitation also needs to be included.

There is no end to the people who need to be visited and worked with that they might be won to Christ and the church.

Therefore many soul-winning programs must be offered by the church.

Three groups of people are usually involved in the outreach ministry of an aggressive, soul-winning church. They are men, women, and young people. Therefore the church should offer various kinds of visitation. There should be a women's visitation, a men's visitation, a teenage soul-winning program, and an all-church general visitation.[16]

The ladies' visitation would normally be held in the mornings for women in the church who do not work outside the home. Some of these may have children in school and the daytime allows them time to get out of the house and do some witnessing for the Lord. The pastor could provide prospect cards for the ladies, meet with them for prayer and devotion, and send them out in pairs. He may want to place a qualified lady in charge at his own discretion.[17]

The men's soul-winning program could be set up as a "Fisherman's Club" where the men work on a trainer-trainee basis. Saturday is usually the best time for this type of visitation because most men do not work on that day. In this program laymen are involved in training laymen to be soul-winners. This could begin each Saturday morning with breakfast at a restaurant or at the church. After the meal, a time of devotions and challenge, and testimonies on soul-winning experiences of the previous week, the men are sent out in pairs for about two to three hours of soul-winning.

Teenage soul-winning is a good program to encourage young people to become witnesses. The program should begin with a training course on soul-winning. Then a kick-off banquet could be held for the teenagers where they are challenged to get involved in the program. The young people fill out commitment cards or faith promise soul-winning cards, and the banquet closes with an announcement of the time of the first teenage soul-winning meeting. Then drivers are enlisted from among the adults who will drive the young people to and from their destinations. Prospects may be obtained from student directories from the various high schools of the city.[18] All the necessary sample forms and instructions needed to organize a teenage soul-winning program can be obtained by writing Rev. Mark Thomas, P.O. Box 1088, Nashville, Tennessee 37202.

An all-church visitation program should be the main visitation program of the church. It should be held at night. Thursday night is the most popular night because it seems to be the best night to find people at home. However, Monday night is an excellent night to call on visitors who attended services the preceding Sunday.

The pastor should spend some real thought, prayer, and time on his all-church visitation program to insure its success. He should be at the church early, have the supplies and the prospect cards ready for team assignment. He should see that each team has some good prospects to visit.

A good devotion and challenge is needed to inspire the people before they go out. A good testimony by someone will help. But there needs to be a time when all the people meet together for prayer, receive their assignments, and all go out together.

The people should be sent out in pairs, but the partners need to be chosen with care. Sometimes husbands and wives prefer to go together. Newcomers to visitation should be sent with more experienced partners.

If someone is discouraged and the pastor knows of a prospect that is ready to be saved, he should send that discouraged person with a good soul-winner and let them lead the prospect to Christ. It will do much to encourage fearful, frightened, discouraged people.

The partners should be instructed to pray together in the car and to make the visits count for Christ. The pastor should make sure that each team fills out the results of the visits on the assignment cards and returns them to the church.[19]

The pastor will constantly need to revise the visitation and soul-winning   programs of the church as new needs arise, but it will pay regular dividends in souls for Christ and new members for the church. Perhaps the new church can begin with only one of the described visitation programs, but the others can be added as the church grows. However, some type of visitation and soul-winning program needs to be offered from the very beginning of the new work.

Follow-Up

When a person visits the church services he should receive a letter from the pastor the following week. This can be a form letter, but one that is personally typed by the church secretary or volunteer worker. This is one reason it is important to get visitors' cards in every service.

The pastor should also visit in the home the following week. The earlier in the week he can go, the better it will be. The person may be unsaved and under conviction from the service he attended. The more quickly he is contacted the easier he can be led to Christ.[20]

The good prospect names should be put in the visitation files so those people can be contacted on visitation during the week. Every effort should be made to win prospects to Christ.

If the person came to Sunday school, the Sunday school teacher should visit the following week. His name should be placed on the mailing list to receive the church paper. If a church will follow this procedure, those who visit the services will be impressed with the friendliness and concern of the church.

Follow-up on those who are saved in church should begin when the converts come down the aisle. There should be trained counselors to meet those who respond to the invitation to deal with them from the Scriptures. A decision card should be filled out and given to the pastor, and a new convert packet containing literature on assurance of salvation should be given the new Christians. These materials may be obtained from the National Home Missions Department, P.O. Box 1088, Nashville, Tennessee 37202.

Each person should be instructed about baptism, and arrangements made to baptize them as soon as possible. A form letter to the new Christians should be sent the following week. The pastor should, by all means, visit each person the following week and take the first lesson of a follow-up series. The National Home Missions Department has these lessons available in a series of thirteen lessons. Every new Christian should be shown how to fill out the answers, and the second lesson left to be worked.

If the church reaches several people, it will be impossible for the pastor to study with all of them. Follow-up workers can be assigned which will alleviate the problem for awhile. But if the church keeps reaching people rapidly, a new class will have to be started at the church, or a full-time man will have to be employed and placed in charge of follow-up.[21]

Rev. Jim McAllister, pastor of the First Free Will Baptist Church, Farmington, Missouri, has a full-time follow-up director. It has enabled their church to keep three out of every four people who have made decisions in their services.

In the beginning, however, a new converts' class, which could also serve as a membership orientation class, would suffice. With thirteen lessons, the courses could be taught perpetually and the new Christians would enter the class the Sunday morning following their conversions. After completion of the thirteen lessons, they would be assigned to their regular Sunday school classes. This kind of new converts' class would constantly be enrolling new pupils and turning out new graduates to be added to the Sunday school and church.

Not only should new converts be urged to complete the thirteen follow-up lessons, but they should be encouraged to become soul-winners. New converts should be encouraged to attend one of the visitation programs and be just silent partners at first.

Follow-up is the most neglected area of most churches. But the pastor who has a good follow-up program will add members to his church and keep those he adds.

Those won at home need to be encouraged to come to church, make public profession, be baptized, and go through the follow-up lessons. As much time should be spent getting them to church as is spent in leading them to Christ.[22]

Conclusion

Visitation and soul-winning are the least expensive areas of church work, yet they are the most productive. The devil will fight these activities with everything he has. But if the pastor will keep his heart warm and his people visiting, it will keep a constant stream of people coming down the aisles. Through the follow-up programs these will be baptized, added to the church, and developed into soul-winners.

Other people will be attracted to the church because of the good services and souls saved. The church planter will be the pastor of a happy, growing church. He will have a deep settled peace in his soul that he is pleasing the Lord. Therefore, the visitation, soul-winning, and follow-up programs must be included in the pastor's plans for the new church.

Chapter X
Reference Notes

[1]Charles M. Underwood, editor, *Planting the Independent Fundamental Church* (Greenville, South Carolina: Bob Jones University, 1972), p. 59.

[2]*Ibid.*, p. 53.

[3]*Ibid.*, pp. 62-63.

[4]Roy Thomas, *How to Get Visitors' Cards* (Nashville: Free Will Baptist Board of Home Missions, 1974), p. 1.

[5]William A. Powell, *The Urban Church Survey Manual* (Atlanta: Home Mission Board, Southern Baptist Convention, 1972), pp. 96-100.

[6]*Ibid.*

[7]George Godfrey, *How to Win Souls and Influence People for Heaven* (Hammond, Indiana: First Baptist Church, 1973), p. 117.

[8]Underwood, p. 52.

[9]James Kennedy, *Evangelism Explosion* (Wheaton: Tyndale House Publishers, 1970), p. 5.

[10]Godfrey, p. 40.

[11]Kennedy, p. 9.

[12]*Ibid.*

[13]Tom Malone, *The Sunday School Reaching Multitudes* (Murfreesboro, Tennessee: Sword of the Lord Publishers, 1973), pp. 70-80.

[14]Jack Hyles, *The Hyles Visitation Manual* (Hammond, Indiana: Hyles-Anderson Publishers, 1975), p. 170.

[15]Kennedy, p. 12.

[16]*Ibid.*, p. 11.

[17]Hyles, p. 11.

[18]Dave Hyles, *Successful Church Youth Work* (Murfreesboro, Tennessee: Sword of the Lord Publishers, 1976), p. 242.

[19]Curtis Hutson, *Pastors' and Workers' Conference* (Decatur, Georgia: Forrest Hills Baptist Church, n.d.), p. 3.

[20]C. W. Fisk, *Fruit That Remains* (Hammond, Indiana: First Baptist Church, 1975), p. 45.

[21]*Ibid.*

[22]*Ibid.*, p. 43.

CHAPTER XI

OUTREACH MINISTRIES

A church must go outside its four walls if it is to grow. Jesus said, " . . . Go out into the highways and hedges, and compel them to come in, that my house may be filled" (Luke 14:23).

The church should resemble an octopus. The many tentacles of the octopus reach out into every direction so that nothing can escape that comes within its reach. The more outreach ministries a church has, the more people it can reach and the faster it will grow. The two most important outreach ministries, the Sunday school and the soul-winning programs, have already been discussed.

The Bus Ministry

The purpose of the bus ministry is soul-winning. It is, in some men's opinions, the greatest evangelistic tool ever available to the local church.[1]

The man who goes out to plant a church should build a solid financial basis under the church, supply the space for adequate Bible teaching, and then add buses as the church can absorb the children.[2] Without these adequate preparations, the bus ministry will have a difficult time in succeeding.

The reasons for a bus ministry are many. The first of these is to get people saved. Children will ride the buses, accept Christ and take Him home to the parents. Then the parents will come and accept Christ, and the families will no longer ride the buses, but come in their own cars.

A second reason for the bus ministry is to provide transportation for those who would not get to church otherwise. God has particularly blessed the bus ministry because it concentrates on the poor. One of the signs Jesus gave John the Baptist that He was the Messiah was, " . . . the poor have the gospel preached to them" (Matt. 11:5).

A third reason for the bus ministry is to put the local church out knocking doors. There is nothing that will get a church going door-to-door and house-to-house like the bus ministry.[3]

The results of a bus ministry in a church are numerous. Souls will begin to be saved. Attendance will rise. Those who have their eyes on themselves will be able to see others in need. Soul-winners will be developed as people learn to visit and knock doors in order to build the routes. People have an opportunity to serve who could not do anything else in the church. People are brought to church who could not get there any other way. The bus ministry is a training ground for preacher boys to give them the experience in door knocking and soul-winning they will need to build and pastor churches.[4]

The reasons for starting a bus ministry should be settled in the hearts of those responsible before it is begun. The expense, hard work, and problems will doom it to mediocrity or failure if there are not powerful and enduring reasons for maintaining it. Some churches have been greatly disappointed because they started bus ministries for the wrong reasons. The basis for the bus ministry is that it serves as an effective tool to carry out the Great Commission and win people to Christ.[5]

So, the pastor needs to look closely at the liabilities before he begins a bus ministry. The bus ministry is a financial liability and the church should accept it as such. Probably no bus ministry will ever become completely self-supporting.

The children who ride the buses may pose problems by being unruly in the services, destroying and defacing the property, or getting lost. Those who make decisions may not attend services regularly. Space problems may be posed.

The more intensely involved a church becomes in evangelism, the more criticism she will receive. Satan will see to that. Those within the church may pose problems, and those outside may criticize. So the church that goes into the bus ministry should realize that these problems will arise.[6] But used properly and organized effectively, a bus ministry can be a tremendous asset to a church. The church can be a real blessing to many people by the proper use of a bus ministry.

The first thing to do in beginning a bus ministry is to secure as many books as possible on the subject, read them, study them, and become acquainted with the problems and possibilities of this outreach ministry. There are many source materials available today from Christian bookstores.

The next thing to do in beginning a bus ministry is to secure a bus. Used buses are available in every large city. The bus must be licensed and insured. It should be painted and the church's name and address put on it.

Next, a driver is needed. He will need a chauffeur's license. The driver must be a responsible person who will be faithful to the task and careful with the precious cargo he hauls.

A bus captain should be secured next. Being a bus captain calls for more dedication than almost any worker in the church. The bus captain many times is the key to whether the bus ministry will be a success or not. He must be willing to spend a large part of every Saturday in the visitation of his bus route.

He must be willing to rise early on Sunday morning, leave home, and spend the necessary time picking up the children. After church he must take them all home. This means that he will eat his Sunday dinner after others have finished. Pastor and congregation should have the utmost respect for Christian workers who will pay that kind of price to get people under the sound of the gospel.

The next step is to choose the route. Anywhere there is a large concentration of children is a good place to build a bus route. Some likely places are apartment houses, trailer courts, any poor area, schools where students board, areas cut off by freeways or industries, military installations, housing projects, or a nearby town.[7]

The bus ministry is very simple to organize. The materials and supplies needed, other than the buses, are few. Clipboards with triplicate report forms are the essentials, and may be ordered from Beebe Publications, Route 4, Box 227, Ruskin, Florida 33570.

The bus captain should go into an area, go from house-to-house inviting people to ride the bus. When some consent to ride, their names are recorded, and they are told what time the bus will arrive on Sunday morning. The captain is careful to explain to the parents exactly what will happen from the time the children leave their homes until they return. A brochure could be prepared with the information explaining the complete operation of the bus ministry.[8]

Each Saturday the bus captain first visits the regular riders, and then begins to visit other homes to obtain new riders. So a bus captain may visit a hundred or more homes in a single Saturday.

As the bus is returning the children home from church, the

captain can get the names of those who will be attending church on Sunday night. To put forth great effort to get people to come on Sunday morning and then make no effort to get them back for the evening service is inconsistent with teaching faithful attendance to all the services.[9]

Five things are necessary to keep a bus ministry going. First is *motivation.* The pastor must constantly promote the bus ministry from the pulpit. The blessings should be shared with the church family regularly. The pastor should meet with the workers before they go out on both Saturdays and Sundays for prayer and to encourage, challenge, and excite them.[10] For this reason some pastors refuse to have a bus ministry because they are not willing to pay the price.

The second necessity is *promotion.* Contests, promotional ideas, and gifts for riders are necessary to keep interest up and the riders coming. Contests do the same thing for the bus ministry that attendance campaigns do for the church. They generate excitement and motivate people to get out and work.

Third, *a good program on the bus* going to and coming from church to keep the riders interested and behaving is necessary. This takes ingenuity from the bus captain and some additional helpers. Bible stories, quizzes, games, and songs can make the trip an enjoyable learning experience for the riders. The happiest times in some children's lives are those spent on the bus and in the services.

Fourth, *a good teaching program in Sunday school and meaningful children's church services* are essential. The bus ministry has been criticized because some have simply hauled children to church, counted them, and hauled them home. But the purpose of the bus ministry is so children can be taught the Word of God and be won to Christ.

The children brought through a bus ministry have not been reared in church. They will disrupt the worship service if put in with the adults. So a children's church is a must. But the pastor should see that it is a good, exciting church service where children receive the Word of God.[11]

The fifth essential is *visitation*. It takes visitation to build the routes. It takes visitation to keep riders coming. It takes visitation to follow-up in the homes of the children who ride the buses to try to reach the parents for Christ. This follow-up should be done, not only by the bus captains, but the Sunday school teachers of the riders, the deacons, the pastor, and other burdened adults of the church.

The bus ministry is hard work. It is expensive to maintain. It is filled with problems and perplexities. It calls for the best from the workers and tolerance from the church. However, it has probably brought more people to Christ than any evangelistic tool of the twentieth century. As soon as the proper foundation can be laid, the church planter needs to begin a bus ministry.

The Day-Care Center

Christian day-care centers operate as a service to parents with small children who find it necessary to be away from home or who want special training in the early years for their children. Parents are charged a weekly rate for each child placed in the day-care, and children are kept in a clean, safe place with a Christian environment.

The church should not start a day-care program as a money-making project, but as an outreach ministry. The children kept should be taught the Bible, making the reason for its existence Scriptural. Efforts should be made to win the parents to Christ.

Many states have special requirements of day-care centers and some require licensing in order to operate.[12] However, this has been challenged in the courts, and churches have won their cases against state licensing for church operated day-care centers in a number of states.

Before attempting to begin a day-care program in the new church, the pastor should study the state laws governing day-care centers in his particular state. He should visit successful day-care centers in operation in other churches. He should also determine the financial liabilities, the problems, the possibilities, and blessings of a church operated day-care center.

Special supplies and equipment will have to be purchased for the operation of a day-care center by the church. Kitchen equipment and food supplies, beds for nap time, first aid supplies, playground equipment, and school supplies are all needed in the operation of a successful day-care program. Many of the problems, requirements, and blessings of a church operated day-care center will be the same as the Christian school. However, if operated properly, the day-care program is another arm by which the church reaches out to its city to meet the needs of people and reach the lost for Christ.

The Christian School

A Christian school operated by the church is not only an outreach ministry to win the lost to Christ, but a needed training and educational ministry for Christian children. The nation's secular schools are no longer a desirable place for Christian youth to obtain their education.

Secular institutions are now committed to a belief in humanism. Man and his accomplishments are valued as the highest and only goal. The existence of the supernatural is consistently ridiculed and denied by institutions. A school system reflects the value of the society it serves. Therefore, America's humanistic-based schools teach that man is the center of existence and all things are explained by natural terms.

In the public school system there is a denial of any permanent standard of conduct, for each child is encouraged to decide for himself what is right and wrong. Christian children in secular institutions are greatly influenced by the authority of both teachers and textbooks to accept many humanistic ideas, even though such ideas are in direct conflict with Biblical principles.

The results of teaching children that there is no God, no hereafter, and no standards are already being felt. For at least twenty years, the nation's graduates have left school with diminishing skills, lack of purpose, and a sense of aimlessness.

However, there is now an alternative. Christian youth can learn by superior methods in an atmosphere conducive to development of spiritual strength and character. Thousands of Christian schools are operating on the basic belief that there is a personal God and that He is the highest possible reality. Christian teachers, administrators, and parents can now work together with the Holy Spirit to instill within students a belief in God. Christian schools truly reflect Biblical values.

At the Christian school, students benefit from the enforcement of standards of conduct as outlined in the Scriptures. While their friends in secular schools are adrift in a system teaching no absolutes, the Christian student is growing in understanding and practice of Biblical self-control. Christian curriculum reenforces what a student is taught at home, in Sunday school, and from the pulpit. Graduating students go forth with an appreciation of discipline, an understanding of moral values, and a true knowledge of God. They are physically, emotionally, academically, and spiritually confident to face their adult lives. Most importantly, they possess the awareness of the most exciting life mission: service for the Lord Jesus Christ.[13]

There are four main areas where a pastor must familiarize himself before attempting to organize a Christian school. They are: the purposes of a Christian school, the facilities of a Christian school, the financial basis of a Christian school, and the staff and faculty of a Christian school. In finding relevant information about these four major areas, the pastor is well advised to consult a variety of educational resources such as state and local boards of education, state agencies, and existing Christian schools. From these he can obtain information concerning teacher certification, school accreditation and transfer students, materials and textbooks needed, and school laws involving such questions as attendance, zoning, and acreage requirements.

Tax agencies are particularly useful when it comes to questions related to local, state, and federal taxes. The local fire department is able to clarify building codes as well as explain the types of furniture and equipment that are permissible. Health department officials provide instructions on such points as food preparation, sanitation, and related questions.[14]

Christian organizations exist that are designed to aid Christian schools by giving valuable information concerning legal advice, group insurance, Christian textbooks, teacher placement, financial problems, and educational aims. A great deal of information can be gained by the pastor if he will contact one or all of the following: American Association of Christian Schools, 6601 Northwest 167th Street, Hialeah, Florida 33015; the National Association of Christian Schools, Box 550, Wheaton, Illinois 60187; and the National Union of Christian Schools, 865 28th Street Southeast, Grand Rapids, Michigan 49508.

Another organization that can be contacted is the Accelerated Christian Education (ACE), Box 2205, Garland, Texas 75041. This organization can supply information that can be of particular interest to a church starting with a small student body, limited finances, and few teachers. The pastor should also contact the Fellowship of Free Will Baptist Christian Day Schools, Executive Office, P.O. Box 1088, Nashville, Tennessee 37202. This organization can supply a list of Christian schools operated by Free Will Baptist churches that the pastor could visit and observe in order to gain information on starting a school.

After having consulted with as many boards, agencies, organizations, and schools as possible, the pastor and church can begin to lay plans for the establishment of a Christian school. If operated properly, the Christian school can be a means of training Christian students in the principles of the Word of God, and also reaching into the community to win boys, girls, and parents to Christ.

Vacation Bible School

Vacation Bible School is one of the most successful

outreach programs that can be used. The Free Will Baptist Sunday School Department has a complete slate of materials for either a five-day or a ten-day school.

Bible school should be a happy time. It is time for pastor, workers, and children to work and play, to share and grow, and have a wonderful experience together in the Lord.[15] Many Bible schools are held in the daytime, but an evening Bible school can be very effective. Evenings allow parents to bring their children. An adult class can be conducted for those adults not working in the Bible school.[16]

Some tips on Bible school follow.

(1) Plan well in advance. Select workers early. Have a Bible school director, secretary, a refreshment committee, and two workers for each class. Have several planning sessions with workers ahead of time. Attendance and offering goals should be set. For many years churches have designated Vacation Bible School offerings to National Home Missions.

(2) Have a parade on Saturday before the Bible school begins, to publicize it and generate excitement.

(3) Have a dedication of Bible school workers and enroll pupils during the Sunday services.

(4) Have adequate intermissions for refreshments. This time can be scheduled so that each class or department is served refreshments at a different time if there is a space problem.

(5) Have the entire school march in, sing a theme song, and have flag salutes. All of this helps generate excitement for the school.

(6) Give an invitation every day in the closing exercises, but do not pressure children to respond.

(7) A picnic could be held at the close of Bible school.

(8) Have a commencement exercise on the Sunday night

following the Bible school. In this service the gospel should be preached and an invitation given. Vacation Bible School is worthwhile for the commencement exercise alone. Parents will come to church to see their children graduate from Bible school who might not come for other reasons. Through a well planned Vacation Bible School many children and parents can be won to Christ.

Youth Camp

The church planter should provide a youth camp for his young people. If the church is isolated, this will be more difficult, but youth camp is well worth the trouble and expense involved. Usually there is a camp that can be rented where the pastor can take his young people and participate with them. The author had camp for a number of years for the young people in his church even though there were no other Free Will Baptist churches in the state.

The pastor should go with the young people to youth camp and stay until it is over. It will be a week well spent. Young people will be convicted, challenged, and called in the services at camp, and the pastor will need to be present   to counsel with them.

The camp should be publicized well in advance and all the young people of the church encouraged to go. Adults may be asked to financially sponsor young people who could not afford the registration fee. Suggestions for curriculum, policies, required insurance, and activities may be obtained from the Free Will Baptist Sunday School and Church Training Department.

After camp is over, the following Sunday night service could be a special youth service where young people share with the rest of the church the blessings received and the decisions made at camp. Many preachers, missionaries, and Christian workers first found God's will for their lives at youth camp.

Revivals

An important outreach ministry of the church is the revival campaign. An evangelist is invited to the church and services are conducted each night. Many people have been brought to Christ through revival campaigns. Others have visited the church during the revival and are won to Christ later. The following is a schedule of how to prepare and conduct a successful revival campaign.

I. Plan the revival.
   A. Set the date.
   B. Secure the evangelist.
   C. Arrange the special music.
   D. Compile a prospect list of those the church hopes to win.

II. Pray for revival.
   A. Get as many people as possible to pray for the revival.
   B. Challenge Sunday school and CTS classes, bus workers, visitation workers, Woman's Auxiliary, and other groups to pray.
   C. Special prayer meetings may be scheduled.
   D. Compose a prayer list and pray specifically for those.

III. Publicize for revival.
   A. Put ads in the newspaper.

B. Get spot announcements on the radio.

C. Take advantage of free newspaper stories.

D. Prepare posters for store windows.

E. Print handbills for distribution.

F. Put advertisements on bulletin boards of sister churches, schools, and places of employment.

G. Mail out handbills with the midweek or church paper.

H. Push through announcements from the pulpit.

I. Print a letter to delinquent church members, bus children's parents, and Sunday school absentees and prospects.

J. Organize a telephone committee to have a barrage of calls to people, especially the church membership, prospects, and lost people.

K. Bumper stickers and billboard advertisements can be used effectively for publicity.

IV. Prepare for revival.

A. Schedule good special music for each night. Make sure those singing measure up to the church's standards of dress and musical tastes.

B. Have the song director sing evangelistic, revival-type songs so the singing will be lively.

C. Keep the song service short. Inform special groups of the number of songs they are to sing.

D. Use a revival theme song. Sing a short, peppy chorus, such as "God is so Wonderful" each night.

E. Use the church choirs, ensembles, and soloists.

F. Have greeters at the doors to welcome visitors.

G. Have men in the parking lots to assist.

H. Alert ushers to help people find seats.

I. Get visitors' cards filled out and returned each night.

J. Train some counselors to work with those who respond to the invitation.

K. Prepare for a good offering each night and see that the evangelist is well paid.

L. Put a large banner across the front of the church with a theme or Bible verse.

M. Designate special nights to help the people build the crowds.

   1. Monday night—Pack-a-Pew Night.
   2. Tuesday night—Neighbor Night.
   3. Wednesday night—Sunday School Night.
   4. Thursday night—Family Night.
   5. Friday night—Youth Night.
   6. Saturday night—Super Night.

V. Promote the revival.

A. Contact special groups such as firemen, policemen, boy scouts, Kiwanis, sister churches, city councilmen, school groups, and invite them for a special night in their honor. Many people in such groups are unsaved and will provide good prospects.

B. Print a news sheet to be distributed as people leave the building, telling highlights of the revival and what is planned for the next night, prayer requests, information concerning transportation, biographical sketch of the evangelist, and articles by members about what the revival means to them.

C. Appropriate awards can be given those bringing first time visitors. Have some type of promotion for each Sunday school class and bus route. Get each person involved. Gospel records or Bibles are excellent give-away items.

D. Give away something small to every visitor. Bible markers or pens with the church address on them are good for this.

E. Use the ideas and talents of the people in plays, skits, music, and advertisement. Do not be afraid to be innovative.[17]

The pastor is responsible to plan revivals and secure the evangelist. In order to get the kind of evangelist who can move the people and draw the crowds, one must be scheduled perhaps a year or more in advance. At least two revivals should be conducted each year. If they are well-planned, they can be an outreach for the church that will win many souls to Christ.

Radio and Television Ministries

It is not likely that a church just beginning will be able to afford a television ministry. The pastor should meet the personnel of television stations and take advantage of talk shows and spot announcements that might be available to him free of charge. But cost will probably prevent his having a television program of his own until the church is strong.

However, radio is an effective tool for preaching the gospel and publicizing the new church. Some spot announcements should be purchased to advertise the beginning of the church.

A radio program should be started soon after the services are begun.[18] Expense and opportunities available will dictate what the pastor can do toward buying radio time. He should start small and extend the program as time and funds allow. Perhaps a five minutes program could be started called, "Five Minutes with an Open Bible." This could give listeners many Scriptural truths in a small amount of time if the pastor is well prepared.[19] He might begin with a weekly program and expand to a daily program. He might start with a five minute program and expand to a fifteen minute program. Fifteen minutes each day is probably sufficient for a beginning church.

The program should present a positive message of the gospel and stay away from controversial doctrines. Other churches or preachers should not be criticized. The church services should always be announced, and an address and telephone number given where people can contact the pastor. The pastor's own ministry and the needs of the area will largely determine the format of the program.

Radio programs can be financed by pledges from individual members, offerings on Wednesday nights, or through the church budget. Listeners may also send gifts to help. Through this means of outreach the church can minister to shut-ins and others who may be unable to attend church.

Telephone Ministry

Two types of telephone directories are available in most cities. The regular alphabetical directory is given to anyone who has a telephone. The other is a street address directory. Sometimes these are listed in the yellow pages under one of the following names:

1. Directories

2. Advertising directories
3. Publishers' directories
4. City directories
5. Criss-cross directories
6. Cross reference directories
7. Reverse directories
8. Polk's directories
9. Blue books

The city hall or Chamber of Commerce will know where these directories can be obtained. Once the book is obtained it will have the city listed by house numbers and streets rather than alphabetical listing of names. This directory will reveal the cost of homes, median income of the area, and number of people per unit.[20]

The telephone book could be divided among callers by sections, and each worker given a sample message telling him exactly what to say. In this manner the city can be canvassed by telephone.[21]

A person can canvass three times as many people by telephone as he can door-to-door in the same amount of time. Weather will not hinder the telephone canvasser. He can get into apartment houses and other places that are closed to the door-to-door worker. People will answer the telephone who will not answer the door. The telephone canvasser usually can write more legibly and get more information than the door-to-door canvasser.[22]

The main advantage of telephone canvassing is that many more people can be reached. A church can usually recruit twice as many telephone canvassers as door knockers. Each telephone canvasser can get information on three times as many people as the door knockers. So the telephone survey can reach about six

times as many people as the door-to-door survey.[23] The
National Home Missions Department has instruction sheets
available on how to organize and conduct the telephone survey.

Other Ministries

The opportunities for special ministries are almost unlimited. There are the retarded, the shut-ins, the handicapped, the
incarcerated, alcoholics, minority groups, and many other
neglected people who can be reached with the gospel and
ministered to by the church.[24] The church that loves people
should strive in every way to meet the needs of those who are
hurting and need spiritual help.

One of the most neglected groups of people are the deaf.
These people will never be saved as a result of a radio program,
or an ordinary church service. They will never hear the gospel
until someone gets burdened for them, learns their language,
and takes the gospel to them in the only language they can
understand—sign language. Some dedicated man or woman
could be sent to sign language classes, learn the language, and
begin a deaf ministry in the church. Deaf prospects can be
located through the Department of Welfare and Health agencies.[25]

Tourists are another group that can be ministered to by
the church. Many times motels and hotels will use a local
minister as chaplain, placing his name and telephone number,
along with Bibles, in every room.   The pastor serving as such a
chaplain will have many opportunities to counsel and witness to
guests needing spiritual guidance.

Conclusion

This is a glorious time in which to live and work for God. He has given so many outreach ministries to use in building the church in the twentieth century. The wise pastor will use everything he can to minister to people in every way, using every means at his disposal to reach as many as possible. God will bless these efforts with souls saved and the church will grow.

Chapter XI
Reference Notes

[1]Jim Vineyard and Jerry Falwell, *Winning Souls Through Buses* (Nashville: Impact Books, 1972), p. 90.

[2]Elmer Towns, *Getting a Church Started in the Face of Insurmountable Odds with Limited Resources in Unlikely Circumstances* (Nashville: Impact Books, 1975), p. 67.

[3]Wally Beebe, *All About the Bus Ministry* (Murfreesboro, Tennessee: Sword of the Lord Publishers, 1970), pp. 17-22.

[4]Jack Hyles, *Church Bus Handbook* (Hammond, Indiana: Hyles-Anderson Publishers, 1970), pp. 11-15.

[5]Charles M. Underwood, editor, *Planting the Independent Fundamental Church* (Greenville, South Carolina: Bob Jones University, 1972), p. 133.

[6]Hyles, pp. 15-20.

[7]*Ibid.*, pp. 63-65.

[8]Elmer Towns, *The Successful Sunday School and Teacher's Guidebook* (Carol Stream, Illinois: Creation House, 1976), p. 168. Used by permission.

[9]Underwood, p. 135.

[10]Jack Hyles, *The Hyles Church Manual* (Murfreesboro,

Tennessee: Sword of the Lord Publishers, 1968), p. 162.

[11]Jim Vineyard, *World's Largest Junior Church* (Hammond, Indiana: First Baptist Church, 1974), p. 124.

[12]Fred E. Friend, *Standards for Day Care Centers* (Nashville, Tennessee, Department of Public Welfare, 1973), p. 5.

[13]Donald Howard, editor, *Facts About ACE* (Garland, Texas: Accelerated Christian Education, Inc., 1976), p. 5.

[14]Eugene Workman, editor, "Are You Ready to Start a Christian School?" *Contact* (October, 1975), p. 1.

[15]Jack Hyles, *How to Boost Your Church Attendance* (Grand Rapids: Zondervan Publishing House, 1958), p. 84.

[16]John R. Bisagno, *How to Build an Evangelistic Church* (Nashville: Broadman Press, 1972), p. 122. Used by permission.

[17]Roy Thomas, *How to Prepare for Revival* (Nashville: Free Will Baptist Board of Home Missions, 1977), p. 1.

[18]Towns, *Getting a Church Started*, p. 130.

[19]Lee Lebsack, *Ten at the Top* (Stow, Ohio: New Hope Press, 1974), p. 18.

[20]William A. Powell, *The Urban Church Survey Manual* (Atlanta: Home Mission Board, Southern Baptist Convention, 1972), p. 29.

[21]*Ibid.*, p. 130.

[22]*Ibid.*, p. 26.

[23]*Ibid.*, p. 13.

[24]Jack Hyles, *The Hyles Visitation Manual* (Hammond, Indiana: Hyles-Anderson Publishers, 1975), pp. 111-143.

[25]Towns, *The Successful Sunday School and Teacher's Guidebook*, p. 329.

CHAPTER XII

ADVERTISEMENT AND PUBLICITY

The church must attract the attention of people to its ministry so that it may be able to exert the influence of the gospel upon them. They must be made aware of their need and opportunity of salvation. This is why it is reasonable and right to promote every legitimate method to reach as many souls as possible.[1] If the pastor is an inspiring preacher, and has put together an exciting program, then he needs enthusiastic publicity to cause the church to grow.[2]

The Mail

One of the first things the church planter should get is a third class bulk mailing permit. The church can mail the church paper or unsealed letters on this permit for 2.1 cents per piece, provided they do not weigh more than 2.4 ounces.[3]

The permit costs $40.00 per year plus a $20.00 application fee. A deposit is required at the post office to cover the cost of the initial mailing. A minimum of 200 pieces per mailing is required. This permit may be obtained by making application at the post office.[4]

The initial mailing list can be compiled with names gleaned from the "get acquainted meetings," the visitors to the services, the newcomers list, those enrolled through the *Attack* program, and other sources. The pastor should screen from the list those he knows are not prospects for his church to keep the cost down. Then he should begin a mail ministry geared to reaching the unchurched families on his mailing list.

The first piece of mail these people should receive is a letter announcing the first service of the new church and the inspiring program that is planned. The address of the church, the time of services, the pastor's telephone number, and perhaps his picture should be included.

On Monday morning after the first Sunday's services, the church planter should send out a card, letter, or paper announcing the great things that happened. The plans for next Sunday should be included. If mailed on Monday, the prospects should have it by Wednesday.

This could be the beginning of a midweek paper that would be sent to the mailing list every week. This paper should be attractive, eye-catching, and well printed. If people receive a messy paper with typographical errors and misspelled words, they will judge the church to be poorly organized and the pastor to be incompetent.[5]

The missionary should invest money in a good typewriter and a good mimeograph machine, and see that whoever operates them learns to turn out excellent work. Sloppy, poorly printed materials are poor advertisement for the church and pastor.

Bob Bell, religious editor for the *Nashville Banner*, says that most churches do more harm than good by their mailings. The work is sloppy, the material poorly written, and of no interest to the readers. So the printed material should be well done and the message should be aimed at the unchurched. The purpose of the mailing is to cultivate the interest of people so they will visit the church. The mailing list, which is being added to weekly as visitors attend the services, and as the church contacts people, can be utilized to help keep a constant stream of visitors pouring into the church.[6]

Next, the church planter should have a number of

promotional letters to use. As mentioned earlier, he should already have stationery prepared with matching envelopes. Since the stationery and envelopes are the only advertisement that some people might ever see of the church, it should be attractively printed on good paper stock, with the address and telephone number of the church and the name of the pastor. The church planter will need to get a temporary supply to last until the church moves into its permanent home.[7]

Most promotional letters should be personally typed, but because of the amount that will be needed, the letter to newcomers should be printed in quantity. This letter, printed on church stationery, should be sent to the newcomers immediately upon their arrival in the city. The letter should include a welcome to the city, an expression of interest in their happiness in their new home, and an invitation to the church.[8] A church brochure should be included which will have some things about the church, the schedule of services, and the plan of salvation.

In most large cities, hundreds of people move into the area each month. The church may need to cut the mailing list down to those areas within a twenty minutes driving distance of the church. This can be done by zip code if it is necessary.

Some promotional letters should be typed personally, at least until the church grows larger. The pastor should make some form letters to be used as guides. From these guides, personal letters can be typed on the church stationery.

Every Monday a letter should be sent to those who visited the services the preceding day. Their names and addresses will be taken from the visitors' cards received in the services. The letter should thank them for coming, invite them back, and offer spiritual help if needed.[9] If the visitor is not on the mailing list, his name should be added. Such a sample letter to be sent to visitors is as follows:

Dear Friend:

It was a real joy to have you as our guest at the First Free Will Baptist Church. We sincerely hope that you received a blessing from the services and that you will visit with us as often as possible.

If you do not have a church home, we hope that you will prayerfully consider our church.

I do pray that the Lord will continually bless your life. If I can be of help to you, feel free to call the church office. It would be a joy to be of service to you.[10]

Sincerely,

Pastor

A decision letter should also be typed on Monday and sent to all who made decisions in the church services the preceding Sunday. A sample is as follows:

Dear Friend:

We praise the Lord for your decision for Christ just made in our church, and want to assure you that our prayers and personal interest are with you. Your decision was the beginning of great things for you and for us as we do His will together.

I want to encourage you to read your Bible and pray every day and to attend church regularly. This will help your faith in Christ to continue to grow. If I can be of help to you, feel free to call the church office. I would be happy to be of service to you.

May the Lord bless you as you live for Him.[11]

Sincerely,

Pastor

The pastor should also prepare sample letters for those who make decisions at home and those who unite with the church. He could also have some special "thank you" letters on file for people who do special things for him and special commendation or congratulation letters to those who are honored.

Until the church is able to employ a secretary, the pastor could select qualified people in the congregation who would be willing to do volunteer secretarial work. These could also scan the newspapers each day and send special letters from the church to newlyweds, those who have had a death in the family, those who have had a tragedy such as a fire, and those who are new parents. All of these could be typed from a sample prepared by the pastor, or printed as form letters if the quantities were too great.

The Newspaper

The church planter should take advantage of all the

opportunities available to get the church before the city. Since many area newspapers will carry church news without cost, the pastor should carefully prepare news releases to these of special events. The releases should contain a message geared to generate enthusiasm and excitement over the church program.[12] They should be typed with double spacing, have all names, dates, and items spelled and listed correctly. Mention names in the news releases. People want to read about people, not statistics and boring facts.

It would be very profitable if a church could put a large ad in the major newspapers each week. But since it is so expensive, it is better for a new church on limited finances to occasionally run a large ad than to put a small ad in every week.

Many times it may appear that the church is receiving a very small return from advertising. Thousands must be contacted through advertisement for ten people to respond. However, if one family is won, their tithes will soon pay for the cost of the advertisement. So advertising never costs—it always pays in the long run.[13]

Through means of the mail, radio, and newspaper advertisement a preacher can soon let his city know that he is there and that his church is in the area to win the lost to Christ and meet the needs of the community. People cannot come to the church until they know it is there.

Special events should be put in the newspaper such as revivals, grand openings, or building dedications. Sometimes it is better to have advertisements on pages other than the church page. One should always aim his advertisement at the unchurched.[14] It is so important for a church just beginning to include some money in the budget for advertisement so it can get its ministry before the city.

Radio and Television

Radio and television have been covered as outreach ministries, but a word should be said about them as advertising means. Spot announcements on the radio are sold on the basis of length and number of times the announcement is made. On a Nashville, Tennessee radio station, WWGM, a spot announcement costs $4.80 for 30 seconds, and $6.00 for 60 seconds. These announcements must be made a minimum of 25 times to get these prices. For $120.00 to $150.00 a church could reach thousands of people with a message. The following are samples of spot announcements, the first being 30 seconds in length.

At one time or another most of us have thought about and discussed the subject of demonism. What do you know about the workings of evil spirits? Is there such a thing today as demon possession? What about casting out evil spirits? You need to get sound practical teaching rather than the sordid scenes of a popular movie. Hear our pastor, Rev. James Keating, teach on demonism during the month of April at First Free Will Baptist Church. Bring your Bible and take notes each Sunday morning at 9:45, Templeton and Pearl Streets, Omaha, Nebraska.[15]

The following is a 60 second announcement.

Adults are like children in more ways than one. For instance, children like Sunday school when there is something to hold their interest. It is true with adults, too. Children like to attend

Sunday school at First Free Will Baptist Church because they find much to interest them. Adults also like Sunday school there because vital and helpful subjects are taught by the pastor, Rev. James Keating. For example, the topic to be discussed this Sunday will be exorcism, or the casting out of demons. When did you last hear a Bible lesson on that topic? You might not have the opportunity to hear it taught again for a long time. Why not plan to visit the Pastor's Class this week? Bring your Bible with you and take notes on the important and timely subject of exorcism, the casting out of demons, this Sunday at 9:45 A.M. at the First Free Will Baptist Church, Templeton and Pearl Streets, Omaha, Nebraska.[16]

The average market for a onetime spot announcement during the day on television would cost approximately $150.00, according to Channel 5, WTVF, Nashville, Tennessee. This announcement would last for 30 seconds. So the only people it would reach are those viewing at that 30-second period of time. For this reason, the pastor will need to weigh the matter carefully about how best to spend his advertising money.

Church Signs and Telephone Listings

The church should prepare an attractive, eye-catching, easy-to-read sign to put on the church property for all to see. The time of services and the pastor's name and telephone number should be on it. It should be high enough to be seen, but low enough so as not to be overlooked. The grass should be kept cut around it, and it should be kept in good repair at all times.

There should also be signs put in other places such as the corners of main arteries near the church. Permission will have to be obtained from the property owners, and permits secured from the city to put the signs there. Randall Bookstore, P.O. Box 17306, Nashville, Tennessee 37217, has some attractive signs which can be purchased. Space is available for the directions to the church to be lettered on them. They should be placed so that people can see them from both directions.

Many times a church can rent billboard space for advertisement. Signs can also be put up on the highways leading into the city.

The telephone book is another way to advertise. The church and pastor's name should be listed in both the white and yellow pages. The pastor should be listed as "Reverend" or "Pastor" because that distinguishes him as a minister. Care should be exercised to explain to the telephone company that the Free Will Baptist church is to be listed as a separate denomination and not just another "Baptist" church. In many telephone directories, it may be listed in the yellow pages under "Churches—Baptist—Free Will." If it is not listed as a separate denomination, people might conclude that it belongs to another Baptist denomination.

Miscellaneous Advertising

Handbills can be printed and distributed. Posters advertising special events can be placed in the car windows of church members and in store windows. Community bulletin boards and factory bulletin boards will sometimes allow posters to be displayed.

Motels usually list a church directory in the lobby or in each room. The pastor can see that his church is included in this listing. City buses sell advertisement space many times on the sides and rear, and also on the inside area above the windows. Park benches also are used for advertising by painting signs on the backs and fronts. Loud speakers can be mounted on the tops of cars or trucks and these driven throughout the area, but a permit must be obtained for this in many cases.

The pastor should get some business cards printed to be distributed freely. He must remember to carry them at all times. Also, an attractive church brochure has many uses. Workers can take them on visitation. If people are not at home, the brochure will let them know someone from the church was there.[17] These can also be enclosed in special mailings.

In a new church, the advertisement and publicity rests on the shoulders of the pastor. As the church's public relations man, he must have a good rapport with the people of his city. The following are twelve basic "B's" for publicity.

(1) Be the only person from your church to contact news media. Two members calling the same newspaper editor or church news editor are bound to bring conflict or confusion.

(2) Be quick to establish personal contact with the right persons at each newspaper, radio and television station in your area. (3) Be sure to write everything down. Train your memory, but do not trust it.

(4) Be prompt in meeting every news deadline.

(5) Be legible. Type news releases. Keep an extra copy for

your own files. Date each news release. Double-space all typing.

(6) Be accurate. Double-check dates, names, places before submitting the copy.

(7) Be honest and impartial. Do not exaggerate. Give credit where due.

(8) Be brief. Newspaper space and air time are costly.

(9) Be brave. Do not be afraid to suggest something new from the church for the area. Media people welcome original ideas when they are practical and organized logically.

(10) Be businesslike. Never try to obtain publicity by pressure of friendship or business connections. Never ask when a story will appear. Never ask for clippings.

(11) Be appreciative of all space and time given the church's publicity. The media given freely also have space and time for sale.

(12) Be professional. Members of the press are always invited guests to special events. Never ask them to buy tickets or pay admission for banquets, dinners, and programs.[18]

Conclusion

The twentieth century has been referred to many times as "The Golden Age of the Church." Truly God has given the church more tools to effectively get the gospel out in this century than at any other time in history. The mail, newspapers, telephone, radio, television, billboards, and many other avenues of advertisement and publicity should be used to get the church before the city.

However, the best means of advertisement the church can have is publicity through "word of mouth" by the members. If every member of the church would be "Sunday school and church conscious" everywhere they go, they would be inviting people to church, telling about the exciting program it has to offer, and giving out the gospel of Christ. This is the most effective means of advertisement, and at no financial cost.

Chapter XII
Reference Notes

[1]Charles M. Underwood, editor, *Planting the Independent Fundamental Church* (Greenville, South Carolina: Bob Jones University, 1972), p. 66.

[2]Robert Schuller, *Your Church Has Real Possibilities* (Glendale, California: Regal Books, 1974), p. 144. Used by permission.

[3]William A. Powell, *The Urban Church Survey Manual* (Atlanta: Home Mission Board, Southern Baptist Convention, 1972), p. 75.

[4]*Postal Service Manual* (Washington D. C.: United States Government Printing Office, 1977), p. 130.

[5]Schuller, p. 145.

[6]*Ibid.*

[7]Jack Hyles, *Let's Use Letters and Forms* (Murfreesboro, Tennessee: Sword of the Lord Publishers, 1962), p. 7.

[8]Hyles, p. 10.

[9]*Ibid.*, p. 32.

[10]*Ibid.*, p. 35.

[11]*Ibid.*, p. 37.

[12]Schuller, p. 146.

[13]*Ibid.*, p. 147.

[14]*Ibid.*, p. 148.

[15]Curtis Hutson, *Pastors' and Workers' Conference* (Decatur, Georgia: Forrest Hills Baptist Church, n.d.), p. 182.

[16]*Ibid.*, p. 183.

[17]*Publicity Handbook* (Ft. Worth: Sperry and Hutchinson Company, 1972), pp. 21-23. Used by permission.

[18]*Ibid.*, p. 2.

CHAPTER XIII

THE CHURCH PROGRAM

It is important to advertise, promote, and visit to get people to the services, but the pastor must conduct good services if the people return. Anything worth doing is worth doing well. The pastor should see that everything is done first class.[1]

The pastor is the pastor of the entire church. He should plan the church program to include everyone.[2] Each person has six basic needs. They are evangelism, teaching, training, fellowship, worship, and service. If the pastor will organize his church to meet these needs, people will love him and come to his church.

The Church Calendar

A growing, progressive church that does not have a complete planning calendar is hard to find. A careful calendar will not only list the dates of various activities, but also the dates preparations begin.[3]

The church calendar should be planned throughout the year with the finishing touches put on it in December. There are certain things the pastor knows he will want to have such as the stewardship campaign, two or more revivals, Vacation Bible School, youth camp, missionary conference, and others.

There are certain naturally high attendance days such as Easter and the Sunday before Christmas. These days will not necessarily need special emphasis, as they will naturally have a good attendance.

There are also some natural low days. Memorial Day, Fourth of July weekend, and Labor Day weekend will cause the bottom to drop out of the church attendance unless something is done toward promotion. On these days the pastor will be wise to plan programs and invite guests that will not only keep the people at home, but will bring others in as well. Special planning should also be given to the summer months to defeat the "summer slump."

There are several special holidays each year that lend themselves to promotion. Mother's Day, Father's Day, Fourth of July, Labor Day, and Thanksgiving are all special holidays around which attendance pushes can be built.

There are also some special seasonal days that can be used to the church's advantage. End of school, back to school, Vacation Bible School, youth camp, homecoming day, old fashioned day, the pastor's anniversary, and the church's birthday are some days that every year can help the church build its crowd if properly planned.[4]

The purpose of a church calendar is threefold: first, so the church can have a balanced ministry to all people of all ages; second, so that the program of the church can be spread out evenly throughout the year; and third, to avoid conflicts in activities. If the pastor will put time, thought, and prayer into carefully planning the church calendar, he will know about special emphasis days in time to promote them. Preachers often think of what could be done on a given Sunday too late to do anything about it.

The following sample church calendar is an outline the pastor could use. He will find several things each month which could be emphasized. In addition to this sheet, he will need a regular calendar for the following year so he can fill in the dates with the planned activities.

When he gets the year planned, he should begin planning how he will promote and conduct the various activities, select the dates for special mailings to be sent out, and order needed materials early.

Sample Church Calendar

Month	Special Emphasis	Miscellaneous Activities
January:	Stewardship Campaign Enlistment Month	Youth Week
February:	Soul-Winning Training Teacher Training	Mother-Daughter Banquet Bible College Sunday
March	Spring Enlargement Campaign	Baby Dedication
April:	Easter Services Revival Foreign Missions Sunday	Lord's Supper and Feet Washing Service
May:	Mother's Day Bus Ministry Emphasis Christian Home Emphasis	Graduation Sunday Serviceman's Sunday
June:	Father's Day Vacation Bible School	Senior Citizen's Day Founders Day
July:	God and Country Day National Association	Annual Church Picnic
August:	Youth Camp (Pastor's Vacation)	Annual Business Meeting Church Anniversary Day
September:	Back-to-School Day CTS Promotional Campaign	Miracle Day Promotion Day
October:	Fall Enlargement Campaign Old Fashioned Day	Homecoming Layman's Sunday

| November: | Annual Missionary Conference
Home Missions Sunday | Thanksgiving Service |
| December: | Christmas Activities | Watch Night Service |

The pastor can take this skeleton and build a church calendar to meet the church's needs. The year's church calendar should be displayed and distributed to the membership, and coming activities should be publicized through the church papers and bulletins.

The Worship Services

The most important part of the service is the preaching. "...It pleased God by the foolishness of preaching to save them that believe" (I Cor. 1:21). All that has been said to this point is ultimately to get people under the preaching of the Word of God.

There is much said today about defending the gospel. The gospel does not need to be defended. If God's people will declare it, the gospel will defend itself. Many believe that the Bible needs to be made relevant to people today. Perhaps there is not as much need to change Biblical terminology into everyday language as there is to make people more familiar with the Bible.[5]

Because this portion has been included toward the end of the writing does not mean that it is the least important. God has always used the preaching of His Word under the anointing of the Holy Spirit to bring men to Himself.

The man who is weak in the pulpit will have a difficult time establishing a strong church anywhere. Advertisement and promotion will cause people to come to church the first time, but the preacher will have to feed them from the Word of God or they will not return.

The Sunday morning service is the best attended service of the week. Normally, more unsaved will be present on Sunday morning than at any time during the week. So the Sunday morning church service should be an evangelistic service. Of course the message will have spiritual food and instruction for Christians, but the service should be geared primarily toward reaching the lost for Christ. The pastor and people work all week toward what will happen at this service. The work, prayers, visitation, promotion, and efforts for the entire week all culminate at the morning worship service.

The ushers are an important part of the worship service. They greet visitors and distribute bulletins as the people enter the auditorium. They need to be trained because they are the first people of the church that most visitors meet when they come to church. The ushers are also responsible for getting the visitors to fill out visitors' cards as discussed in chapter ten. The ushers also need to be instructed on how to receive the offerings quickly and smoothly, because there is not the time in the Sunday morning service as in other services. If the preliminaries are too long, the pastor is under pressure to get through preaching on time. People usually grow restless and expect the service to be over around 12:00 o'clock noon. Children's church workers must hold the children until the adult service is over, and this puts a strain on them if this service runs overtime.

Also, time needs to be allowed for the invitation. For the most effective invitation, it needs to begin about ten minutes to twelve. So the service needs to begin on time with everyone in place, including the choir and Sunday school workers, and progress steadily toward the climax.

The public invitation is the most important part of the worship service.[6] Many souls are lost and churches are stunted because of an ineffective invitation. A farmer may lose a crop because of poor planning for the harvest. A salesman may be unable to sell his product unless he learns to close the sale. The following are some suggestions which may be adapted to the church as the pastor sees fit.

I. Give the invitation.
   A. Include the unsaved.
      1. Tell them specifically what to do. ("Get out of your seat, walk down the aisle. Someone will meet you, kneel with you and show you just what to do, or they will accompany you to the prayer room.")
      2. Ask each to raise his hand while heads are bowed in prayer.
         a. They make a start toward being saved.
         b. They admit they are lost and want to be saved.
         c. It lets the preacher know whom God is convicting.
   B. Include others.
      1. Invitations should include the backslider.
      2. A call for special service such as missionaries, preachers, and soul-winners should be included.
      3. A response to a particular message may be desired. (For a tithing message, appeal for those who will tithe.)
II. The music should be appropriate.
   A. The musicians should be trained.
      1. The musicians and song director should automatically know when to begin.

      2. If musicians play through prayers, it should be done softly.

      3. The song director should watch the preacher to know when to stop or begin a verse.

  B. The singing should not distract.

      1. Use either choir or congregational singing.

      2. Use appropriate, familiar invitation hymns.

III. Going to people in the congregation during the invitation should be done with caution.

  A. Some problems can arise from this practice.

      1. It may embarrass people.

      2. Many get angry and will not come back to church.

      3. It sometimes gives the church a reputation so that others will not attend.

      4. It results in some people going forward before they are ready.

      5. It many times encourages the wrong people to go to the unsaved in the congregation.

      6. It may be attempting to do the work of the Holy Spirit.

  B. It may be done in some situations.

      1. Encourage Christians to sit beside those they are concerned about.

      2. Approach a person from behind so as not to attract attention.(Be sure the Holy Spirit is leading you.)

IV. Use trained altar workers.

  A. Do not pray loudly at the altar. This hinders the invitation.

B. The pastor should stay at the pulpit to extend the invitation. Let others work with those at the altar.

C. Make sure each one who comes forward has someone to deal with him.

D. Make use of prayer rooms for those who need further counseling or anyone wishing to go there.

Altar workers should be trained to meet the person at the front and assist him with his decision. The following is an outline to use in training altar workers.

Introduction:

A. Come to the services praying and expecting to see souls saved.

B. Come hoping and praying that God will use YOU in the service.

C. Be concerned about your appearance, cleanliness, and breath.

D. Sit with or near those in spiritual need and pray for them during the service.

E. Casually observe these prospects during the service and the invitation.

F. If led, speak to them during the invitation or after the benediction.

G. Be ready to respond immediately when needed at the altar.

I. Be wise in the approach.

A. Deal according to sex and age when possible.

B. After introducing yourself, get his name and use it.

C. Determine his need by asking him why he came.

   D. Remember, he is already under conviction. He is ready to
      do something now.

 II. Be wise in dealing with the backslider.
   A. Ask him if he knows why he drifted from God. It is not
      necessary for him to tell the counselor, but he must tell
      God.
   B. Show him I John 1:9 and explain its meaning.
   C. Ask him if he believes the verse and is willing to do as it
      says right now.
   D. Lead in a very brief and simple prayer.
   E. Have him pray. Help him if necessary.
   F. Then pray again thanking God for what He has done.
   G. Review I John 1:9 for assurance.

III. Be wise in dealing with the lost.
   A. Ask him if he knows that he is lost and that Jesus died
      for his sins.
   B. Use Romans 10:9 and explain the meaning.
   C. Ask him if he believes the verse and is willing to do as it
      says right now.
   D. Lead in a very brief and simple prayer.
   E. Have him pray. Help him if necessary.
   F. Then pray again thanking God for what He has done.
   G. Use I John 5:13 and Revelation 3:20 for assurance.

Conclusion:
   A. Final instructions are given.

1. Make sure he has assurance.
2. Fill out a decision card and give him the follow-up material.
3. Encourage the new convert to do the following:
   (a) Record his spiritual "birthday" on the New Birth Certificate found in the follow-up material.
   (b) Tell someone about his conversion as soon as possible.
   (c) Read the Bible daily.
   (d) Study the follow-up material until completed.
   (e) Pray daily.
   (f) Be baptized as soon as possible.
   (g) Join and faithfully attend a good Bible believing church.
4. Introduce him to the pastor.
5. Introduce him to others in the congregation after services are over.
6. Continue with him through the complete follow-up program as explained in Chapter X.

B. Avoid some things.
1. Avoid taking too much time at the altar. Do not talk him out of conviction.
2. Avoid using too many Bible verses.
3. Avoid attempting a case beyond your abilities.
4. Avoid feeding anyone at the altar the "meat" of the Word of God.

The Sunday morning or evening service is a good time for the baptismal services. Many baptize at the end of the service, but the baptismal service can be included in the song service very effectively. Baptismal robes must be provided for the candidates, as well as towels, hair dryers, and dressing rooms. This keeps the candidates from having to bring extra clothes to the service. Also candidates could be baptized immediately upon conversion. The pastor could use a baptismal robe and waders underneath to avoid having to change clothes. With these necessary items the candidates can prepare for baptism when the song service begins. After opening the service, the pastor can go and prepare. With the use of waders and a robe, he can be in the baptistry ready to baptize in the time it takes to sing one song.

After the baptismal service is over, the pastor can be back in the auditorium during the next song. The candidates can dress, use the hair dryers, and be back in the service by the time the sermon begins. The candidates should be aided by the deacons and their wives from the time they leave to prepare for baptism until they return to the auditorium.

The Sunday evening service is conducted much like the Sunday morning service. Usually there is more time so the sermon can be somewhat longer, and more time can be given for singing, announcements, promotion, and prayer.

The Sunday evening sermon should be given primarily to exhorting the Christians and instructing the saints.[7] Sunday night is a good time to take a book in the Bible and preach through it in a weekly series. An invitation should always be given at the conclusion of the service.

The pastor should plan well for the Wednesday evening service also. It should be a time that is dedicated primarily to teaching, from the standpoint of the pastor's message. Bible doctrine could be taught through a series from the *Treatise* or the Church Covenant. The pastor should be in charge of the service. An invitation should be given if the pastor feels a need.[8]

Wednesday night is a good time to have a "missionary of the week" presentation.[9] Each week a different person from the congregation could be assigned to report on a mission field or a particular missionary. An offering could be taken for that missionary. In the course of a year's time, the church would have given to each foreign and home missionary and prayed for each one. Members could obtain information for these reports by writing to the missions departments or to the missionaries personally.

Worship services should be well planned, but informal. Formal, ritualistic services are unscriptural. "Gloria Patri" and the "Sevenfold Amen" do not speak to the hearts of men. There should not be "Sunday morning songs" and "Sunday night songs," but familiar hymns for both services. People come to church from problems and misery. They need to be able to forget their troubles and get their eyes on Jesus and Heaven. When they go home, they should feel as if they have been to church, not a funeral.[10]

The musicians should be at their places and play familiar hymns about ten minutes before the services. The services should always start on time. This tells those present that the church is not only efficient, but also using time wisely.

Not all songs in hymnbooks are the kind to use while building a new church. The pastor should go through the book and mark the appropriate songs for the music director. In this way the director can have the liberty of selecting the songs for the service, but he picks them from the list of appropriate songs. The pastor should also mark the invitation hymns he wants used.

An order of service should be made out ahead of time so that the pianist, organist, choir leader, pastor, ushers, and other workers know exactly what will happen. The page numbers of the songs should be included. Copies of the order of service should be given to all having a part in the service.

The song leader should introduce the songs clearly and remember that his job is to lead the singing, not give a talk before each song. A familiar hymn should be played during the offering. Special music should be well prepared, with the pastor making sure that those singing measure up to the church's standards of dress and musical tastes.

The musicians and song director should take their places during the prayer before the invitation. They should do this automatically without the pastor having to ask them to come forward. The organist and pianist should start playing softly immediately upon arrival at the instruments, and play continuously unless stopped by the pastor. No one should change the invitation hymn after it is begun but the pastor.[11] Following the closing prayer the musicians should play a hymn as the people leave the building.[12]

Many times the choir has been cleverly labeled as the "war department" of the church. There are many fine musicians who are capable, godly, and humble. Unfortunately, there are also some who are the opposite of this. Those used in the music program in the church should be faithful Christians who dress and act accordingly.[13]

The Church Nursery

A beautiful, clean, well-organized nursery is very necessary in a new church. It makes a good impression upon visitors, eliminates disturbances from the church services, frees mothers to work in the church, and allows visitors to hear the message so they can be saved.

It can be started by securing baby beds or cribs, sheets, tissues, baby powder, disposable diapers, washcloths, crackers, plastic bags, and waste cans. Until full-time nursery workers can be employed, it can be operated by the women of the church taking turns. A nursery director may be appointed to see that workers are present and everything is in order for each service. Uniforms should be provided for the workers.

The children need to be separated by age (infants from toddlers) and a method should be developed to identify each baby with its belongings. No one should be allowed in the nursery except babies and workers.

The rooms must be kept neat and clean, and all toys used for toddlers should be safe and sterilized. If possible the floors should be carpeted. The workers need to be present at least fifteen minutes before the services start, and should not accept children into the nursery who are ill.

Parents should be encouraged to use the nursery, and appreciation should be shown for the workers. Dr. Jack Hyles in his book, *The Hyles Church Manual,* has many helpful suggestions for the operation of a successful church nursery.

Children's Churches

Although children's churches are essential to an effective bus ministry, starting them just to rid the worship services of unruly children is the wrong motive for their beginning. There should be children's churches because God's Word can more effectively be preached to one age span of persons than can be done by covering several ages.

Children can be more effectively preached to and dealt

with resulting in more being saved in children's churches. On the other hand, more sinners are saved in the adult service because they are not distracted by children misbehaving in the service.[14]

Sometimes a children's church is needed because of a lack of available space in the main auditorium. This enables a church to grow larger and get more members before building a new auditorium.

In order to have an effective children's church there must be a competent director who can hold the interest of the children and maintain discipline while presenting the gospel to them. There also needs to be a pianist, song leader, helpers, and counselors.[15]

The rooms where the children's churches meet can be decorated and furnished attractively with the needs of children in mind. A puppet ministry can be used very effectively in teaching the Word of God. The book, *Welcome to the Backyard*, contains needed information for organizing children's churches and also directions on how to make puppets.[16] The puppets and other children's church supplies can be purchased in Sunday school supply houses and Christian bookstores. A good variety of puppets can be ordered from Western Oaks Baptist Church, 2800 North Divis, Bethany, Oklahoma 73008 or from Randall Bookstore.

The pastor needs to organize and oversee the children's churches carefully and make sure that the needs of the children are being met. Many children can be won to Christ and trained in the Word of God if children's churches are operated efficiently and effectively.

Youth Ministries

If a preacher can build a good youth program and win the hearts of the teenagers, they will spread excitement through the whole church. Every public service is a youth activity and young people should look forward to participating in each one.[17] Each young person is an individual different from all others, but young people have eight basic needs. The youth program of the church should try to meet these eight basic needs.

The *spiritual need* is first. Young people need to be convicted of sin and then converted to Christ. Then they need to be taught God's Word so they can be built up in the faith to resist the temptations of the devil and win others to Christ. Sunday school, Church Training, visitation, the bus ministry, and teenage soul-winning are all activities that will help do this.

There is a *mental need.* Young people's minds are sharp and they learn rapidly. This is the time to get them to hide God's Word in their hearts through Scripture memorization. The Sword Drill, Tic-Tac-Toe, and Bible Bowl activities of the Sunday School and Church Training Department are excellent for this.

The *physical needs* of young people must be met. Many churches, especially those with Christian schools, are erecting gymnasiums to help meet the physical needs of young people. Many churches have sports programs, not only as outreach programs to win the lost, but to provide competitive activities with youth groups from sister churches.

Young people have *social needs* that the church can help meet. Of course, these must be Christian and chaperoned, but there should be regular activities scheduled, as well as very special events, such as an annual sweetheart banquet or senior trip. Responsible people need to be put in charge of the youth program, and rules need to be carefully drawn up to govern all events concerning conduct, apparel, and dating.

A *musical need* also exists in young people. God placed in young people musical talents that the church needs. If the church will use these talents and get the young people involved in using their music for the Lord, they will not get involved in the world's music. Young people should be encouraged to take music lessons and learn to play instruments. They should be encouraged to participate in the youth choirs, ensembles, and all musical activities. Again the Sunday School and Church Training Department meets this need through its Music and Arts Festival in the competitive activities at the National Youth Conference meeting with the National Association of Free Will Baptists each year. The pastor should urge his young people to participate.

There is also a *cultural need* among young people. One of the problems in America today is that there is very little real refinement and good culture. This is one reason why many people are unhappy. Young people need to have some things which are appropriate. They need to be taught manners and how to conduct themselves in any situation. The *Christian Charm Course* for girls [18] and *Man in Demand* for boys[19] are excellent to help meet the cultural needs. They can be ordered from Randall Bookstore, P.O. Box 17306, Nashville, Tennessee 37217. These courses could be taught through the Church Training on Sunday or Wednesday nights.

Everyone has *personal needs* which can only be met through a daily walk with the Lord. "Conscious Christian Living" is a course in Christian discipline which young people can use for daily devotions, Bible memorization, and prayer life. This course can be ordered from First Baptist Church, 523 Sibley Street, Hammond, Indiana 46320.

Young people have *emotional needs.* Good warm Spirit-filled services at church will certainly give release to built-up emotions and strength to face the temptations at school the next week.[20] The church should provide opportunity for young people to love lost souls, weep over people who are without Christ, and express emotion over things of God. The Christian life is not entirely emotionalism, but emotionalism comes as a result of the Christian life.

A complete youth program is simply the fulfillment of the needs of human beings. The pastor must realize that the basis of working with teenagers is meeting each teenager's needs on his level and replacing the things of the world with the things of Christ and of the Bible. The preacher who will seek to meet these needs in his young people will gather about him a band of workers who will do anything he wants done.

Church Training Service

The training part of the church is very important. Deacons, ushers, altar workers, soul-winners, teachers, and others need to be trained. If the church is to have faithful workers, it must train them, not only to know what their jobs are, but how to do them.

Much has been said in other chapters about training of deacons, soul-winners, church officers, and staff. However, an effective Church Training program needs to be established in the church to train all who come to know Christ. The Sunday School and Church Training Department, P.O. Box 17306,

Nashville, Tennessee 37217, has sample constitutions and bylaws and guidebooks needed for setting up an effective Church Training program. This department also has literature for class instruction for all ages, needed supplies for all competitive activities, and study courses on elective subjects.

The Church Training hour can be used to train ushers, deacons, and other church officers how to effectively do their jobs. Some churches use this time to train choirs and other musical ensembles. Many churches also use the Church Training hour for teacher training courses. Courses on soul-winning can also be taught during the Church Training hour. If a church wants to see its people develop into mature, responsible Christians who go forth to win others to Christ, it must have an effective training program to meet these needs.

Prayer

The church planter must be a man of prayer if he is successful. Prayer brings the presence of God into human endeavors. God makes the difference between success and failure.

Prayer is an important key to church growth. It should begin with the pastor's own personal prayer life. There should be regular times of prayer and fasting in his life for the Holy Spirit's power to be on his ministry. If he prays, his people will follow his example.[21]

There should be prayer in all the services. Much of the midweek service should be given to prayer. The pastor should pray with his teachers and officers when he meets with them in their weekly meetings. He should pray with his bus workers each week before they go out on visitation. He should pray with the soul-winners each week at the different visitation programs of the church. Deacons, trustees, and any other groups who meet together should be taught to pray.

Some churches have an early morning prayer meeting each day before the people go to work, or a Saturday night men's prayer meeting. Other churches have an "early bird's prayer meeting" on Sunday mornings before Sunday school. The pastor and deacons could meet together for prayer between Sunday school and the worship services, which will draw them closer together. Many churches use prayer rooms where men, women, and young people may gather for a few minutes of prayer before the worship services.

In special times of need, such as revivals, building programs, missionary conferences, or sickness, all-night prayer meetings should be scheduled. People can be challenged to pray at a given hour during the day, or take turns praying around the clock.

The pastor must take the lead and keep the church praying. Laborers and workers will come in answer to prayer. Needs will be met and souls saved as the church prays. If the church planter wants to build a growing, soul-winning church for the glory of God, he must realize the importance of the power of the Holy Spirit on his ministry and life through prayer.

Fellowship

Fellowship is an important part of a church program. Churches are held together by love. In a new church the people usually are not acquainted. The church can never be strong until the members of the church get to know each other and are bound together by cords of love.

The church needs to have fellowship dinners or potluck suppers where the entire congregation eats together. There should be banquets, perhaps in restaurants rather than the church, for very special occasions. There could be an annual church picnic, weekend retreats, camping trips, and sports activities to promote fellowship among the members. There is no end to opportunities for fellowship, and the pastor should draw his church around him by loving his people and fellowshipping with them. People's hearts are hungry for love and acceptance. The church can meet these needs. New members, especially, should be welcomed into the fellowship of the believers and be made a part of the congregation and its activities.

Missionary Conferences

The church should have an annual missionary conference, starting from the first year of the church's existence, where missionaries are brought in and people are challenged to prayer and support of missions through the faith promise plan. The following is an outline the pastor can follow in planning the missionary conference. It should include both home and foreign missions, because the church must be taught to have a worldwide vision.

I. The *purpose* is to obey Christ.
   A. He gave the Great Commission.

    1. His program is outlined (Acts 1:8).

    2. His program is explained.

      a. Jerusalem was their city.

      b. All Judaea was their state.

      c. Samaria represented the rest of their country.

      d. The uttermost part of the earth was the rest of the world.

  B. The church is to carry out the Great Commission.

    1. A church should be engaged in preaching the gospel to the world.

    2. This includes its city, its state, its country, and the foreign fields.

II. The *pastor* is the key.

  A. He is the overseer of the church (Acts 20:28).

    1. He must see the need of the church being involved in a worldwide outreach.

    2. He must lead the church in a missions program that reaches the whole world.

  B. He is to involve the church.

    1. He sets the example.

      a. He believes in the Great Commission.

      b. He personally prays and gives to support missionaries.

    2. He teaches his people to get involved.

      a. He acquaints his people with the missions program.

      b. He encourages prayer support.

      c. He challenges them to give.

III. The *people* are to get involved.

  A. They are to send.

      1. "And how shall they preach, except they be sent . . . " (Romans 10:15).

      2. The church is to send those the Lord has called (Acts 13:2, 3).

    B. They receive a blessing.

      1. They lay up treasures in Heaven (Matt. 6:19, 20).

      2. Their missionary gifts are recorded in Heaven (Phil. 4:17).

      3. They have a part in getting souls saved.

IV. The *plan* must be clear.

    A. An annual conference should be scheduled.

      1. The missionaries need to be committed through the Home and Foreign Missions offices, P.O. Box 1088, Nashville, Tennessee 37202.

      2. The dates should be set.

    B. The pastor should push for good attendance and involvement.

      1. Prayer meetings should be held.

      2. Advertisement should be used. (If a church will push its missions conference as it does its revivals, the conference will be successful.)

V. The *promotion* must be thorough.

    A. Publicize the conference.

      1. Preach several sermons on missions.

      2. Push the conference from the pulpit.

      3. Pray for it in the services.

      4. Put the announcements in the church midweek paper and in the newspapers.

      5. Place posters on bulletin boards, advertise in bulletins, have exhibits of missions materials, and put up a large banner in the church.

      6. Pin a personal letter out of the pastor's heart just before the conference and mail to the membership.

B. Put up a goal.

    1. Set the goal carefully.

      a. Include an amount from each auxiliary organization of the church.

      b. Include some from the church budget.

      c. Estimate the cash offerings.

      d. Figure some faith promises from each family in the church.

    2. Total these figures and come up with a goal for the year.

      a. Put this goal where people can see it.

      b. A thermometer is a good way to display the goal.

VI. The *procedure* should be well-planned.

A. Make the services lively.

    1. Watch the length.

    2. Use missionary songs.

    3. Have good special music.

    4. Alert the speakers of your goals and aims.

    5. If visual equipment is used, have it checked and ready.

    6. Aim the service at people's hearts.

B. Prepare to receive the faith promises.

    1. Prepare a large decorated box for people to drop in their faith promise cards or sheets.

    2. Prepare faith promise sheets with the names of the missionaries the church plans to support. Include amount of quota and blanks for the people to indicate their faith promises to various missionaries. (See sample faith promise sheet.)

3. Take the faith promises on Sunday if possible.
   a. Instruct the children (junior age and up) and adults in a combined class during the Sunday school.
   b. Take faith promises during the morning worship service.
   c. Take them again on Sunday evening.
   d. Keep excitement building by announcing the total faith promises as they come in.
   e. Announce the total and rejoice with the congregation.

VII. *Perpetuate* the missionary spirit throughout the year.
  A. Set one Sunday per month as "Missions Sunday."
    1. The first Sunday of the month is usually best.
    2. Make a poster to display in the front of the auditorium.
     a. On one side put, "Next Sunday is Missions Sunday. Remember your faith promises."
     b. On the other side put, "Today is Missions Sunday. Remember your faith promises."
  B. Use missions offering envelopes.
    1. Keep a supply in the church.
    2. Those who fill out faith promise cards or sheets will be sent envelopes by the missions departments.
  C. Plan for next year.
    1. Review your progress.
     a. How much has been given?
     b. How have the church finances been affected by the giving to missions?
    2. Encourage the people to renew their faith promises.
    3. Encourage the people to raise their faith promises.

(Sample Faith Promise Sheet)
First Free Will Baptist Church
Annual Missionary Conference
"Every Member Involved in World Evangelism"
"No one can do it all, but all can do something!"
What You Should Know About The Missionary Conference
March 22-26, 1978, Wednesday Evening—Sunday Evening
NEXT WEEK begins the ANNUAL MISSIONARY CONFER-
ENCE! The church will seek to raise by faith the needed prayer
and financial support for several missionaries. PLEASE make it
a matter of personal prayer *now* as to what you and your
family, under God, will do for WORLD EVANGELISM through
your church during the Missionary Conference. Listed here are
several missionary causes needing support. WILL YOU SHARE
WITH THEM MONTHLY?

MISSIONARY	FIELD	YOUR GIFT
Charles Harris	Northglenn, Colorado	_____
Mark Vandivort	Flagstaff, Arizona	_____
Harley Bennett	Pocatello, Idaho	_____
Bobby Aycock	Brazil	_____
Dr. Laverne Miley	Africa	_____
Don Sexton	France	_____
Other:		
_____	_____	_____
_____	_____	_____
_____	_____	_____

THE CHURCH ASKS YOU TO DO SEVEN (7) SIMPLE
THINGS:

1. Please make the entire Missionary Conference a matter
of real prayer.

2. Let the Lord help you determine what you can give.
   Then trust Him.
3. Plan to attend every service of the Missionary Conference this year.
4. Renew your past financial commitment to the above
   missionaries.
5. Make your *faith commitment* known during this conference.
6. If it is impossible for you to attend the Missionary
   Conference, MAIL IN YOUR COMMITMENT.
7. Continue to pray and give faithfully the next twelve
   (12) months.

Signed:_____

The missionaries should be well cared for during their stay
at the church and sent on their way rejoicing in the blessings of
God. The church will also be blessed for obeying the Great
Commission.

Business Meetings

Some churches have monthly business meetings while
others find quarterly conferences are sufficient. However, short
monthly business meetings may be needed to receive new
members into the church. A lot of the business can be
eliminated by printing reports and distributing them to the
congregation. The people have the information in hand and the
reports do not have to be read orally.

The pastor should meet with the advisory board before

each business meeting. He should have a regular agenda drawn up of items he wishes to bring before the board for discussion. The discussion should be carried on in a businesslike manner. Each board member should have the right to express his opinion, but care should be taken that no one dominates the meeting. A vote should be taken on each item to be recommended to the church. A unanimous vote should be sought, especially on items of major importance. The meeting should be conducted in the spirit of Christ, giving place to the leadership of the Holy Spirit in all things.[22]

Since the advisory board is simply advisory in nature, matters should be decided by vote of the church, but bringing things to the board will mean that items are discussed and prayed about by the leaders of the church. With the main leadership in agreement, the pastor will have no trouble getting the church's approval.

Usually the best time for business meetings is on Wednesday nights after the services are completed. The people are there and in a good spiritual frame of mind. The pastor should gather facts to support what he believes the Lord is leading him to do so that he can answer the questions that may be posed. Ample time should be allowed for discussion and questions, but the meeting should not be long and drawn out to where it is tiring on the people.[23]

No business meeting should be held without the pastor, and major items should be announced two weeks in advance. The treasurer's report should be distributed and the clerk's report should be read orally. Deacons and other boards and committees should have reports ready. If business meetings are properly planned, the business can be expedited quickly and smoothly causing the church to work together in harmony.

Annual business meetings can also be conducted efficiently if all officers have their reports ready and if the nominating committee has done its work.

The Lord's Supper and Feet Washing Services

Regular times should be set for the observance of these gospel ordinances at the discretion of the church and pastor. However, they should be observed at least once each year. Many churches observe them annually on Palm Sunday or Easter Sunday evening.

Preparation should be made beforehand for these services by securing the sacraments of grape juice and unleavened bread. Unleavened bread may be obtained from a Christian bookstore. The communion sets should be washed and glasses filled prior to the service. These sacraments should be placed on the communion table and covered before the service begins. The pastor should carefully plan an order of service and conduct it with reverence and dignity.

At the conclusion of the communion service, the congregation is divided by the sexes for the observance of the feet washing service, with the men and boys in a different part of the church building from the women and girls. This service should be conducted with reverence and humility. Basins, towels, and sufficient amounts of warm water should be supplied both groups.

Auxiliary Organizations and Their Programs

Woman's Auxiliary and Master's Men groups may be

formed as auxiliary organizations to the church, each operating under its own constitution and bylaws under the approval of the church. By sponsoring study courses, missions projects, soul-winning projects, and benevolent activities, these organizations assist the church in obeying the Great Commission. Manuals and guidebooks may be ordered from Woman's National Auxiliary Convention, P.O. Box 1088, Nashville, Tennessee 37202, and Master's Men, P.O. Box 17306, Nashville, Tennessee 37217.

Conclusion

If the pastor wants a soul-winning church, he must make soul-winning the most important emphasis in the church program. Nothing should be allowed to take the place of or interfere with this soul-winning emphasis.

The church program should be so arranged that people's time is not all taken by the church. Services should be planned with care, and auxiliaries should be guarded so as not to involve the people too many nights in the week. People should have time to spend at home with their families.

Meetings should not be scheduled frequently that take different family members away from home every night of the week so that there is no time to be together. The church will be strong only as families are strong. Therefore, the church program should not be so complex as to rob people of family life.

The church should strive, however, to have a total church program that will meet the needs of every family member. Through warm, evangelistic worship services, prayer meetings, children's churches, youth activities, Sunday school, Church Training, and soul-winning activities, the needs of parents, boys, and girls will be met. A total church program will equip the saints to "do the work of the ministry ."

Chapter XIII
Reference Notes

[1]Charles M. Underwood, editor, *Planting the Independent Fundamental Church* (Greenville, South Carolina: Bob Jones University, 1972), p. 166.

[2]Bernard Palmer, *Pattern for a Total Church* (Wheaton: Victor Books, 1975), p. 29.

[3]Harold J. Westing, *Make Your Sunday School Grow Through Evaluation* (Wheaton: Victor Books, 1976), p. 50.

[4]Jack Hyles, *The Hyles Church Manual* (Murfreesboro, Tennessee: Sword of the Lord Publishers, 1968), pp. 124-127.

[5]John Bisagno, *How to Build an Evangelistic Church* (Nashville: Broadman Press, 1972), p. 67. Used by permission.

[6]Hyles, p. 303.

[7]*Ibid.*, p. 289.

[8]*Ibid.*, p. 314.

[9]*Ibid.*

[10]Jack Hyles, *Let's Build an Evangelistic Church* (Murfreesboro, Tennessee: Sword of the Lord Publishers, 1962), p. 84.

[11]George Godfrey, *Helps to Have a Soul Winning Church* (Crown Point, Indiana: Hyles-Anderson College, 1976), pp. 82-98.

[12]Elaine Colsten, *As I See Church Music* (Hammond,

Indiana: Hyles-Anderson Publishers, 1969), p. 31.

[13]Underwood, p. 23.

[14]Jim Vineyard, *World's Largest Junior Church* (Hammond, Indiana: First Baptist Church, 1974), pp. 1-9.

[15]Curtis Hutson, *Pastors' and Workers' Conference* (Decatur, Georgia: Forrest Hills Baptist Church, n.d.), p. 20..

[16]Paul C. Brunner, *Welcome to the Backyard* (Wilson, North Carolina: Peace Free Will Baptist Church, 1977), p. 28.

[17]Hyles, *The Hyles Church Manual*, p. 175.

[18]Emily Hunter, *Christian Charm Course* (Portland, Oregon: Manna Publications, 1975), p. 3.

[19]Wayne Hunter, *Man in Demand* (Portland, Oregon: Manna Publications, 1975), p. 3.

[20]Dave Hyles, *Successful Church Youth Work* (Murfreesboro, Tennessee: Sword of the Lord Publishers, 1976), pp. 37-40.

[21]Lee Lebsack, *Ten at the Top* (Stow, Ohio: New Hope Press, 1974), p. 35.

[22]Melvin Hodges, *A Guide to Church Planting* (Chicago: Moody Press, 1973), p. 62. Used by permission.

[23]Hyles, *The Hyles Church Manual*, p. 14.

CONCLUSION

The purpose of this writing has been to give the details needed in planting and growing a fundamental church. A step-by-step procedure has been described beginning with the call of the worker, his moving to the city, the starting of services, the organizing of the church, its becoming self-supporting, and continuation to become a strong influence for God in its city.

Not all the suggestions here can be used by every church planter. Each must take the suggestions and adapt them to his own particular situation. Each will need to add programs as the work grows.

More could be said on every subject discussed. Time and space do not permit a more detailed coverage of the material. A framework has been given around which the church planter can build his own program. The reference notes for each chapter are placed at the end of that chapter. This is so the church planter can have the books needed for a more detailed explanation of the subjects covered in the chapter.

It is hoped that God will direct the material covered here to men who will give their lives to planting and growing Free Will Baptist churches. This will result in people hearing about Jesus Christ, coming to know Him as Saviour and Lord, and serving Him in bringing others to Christ and the Free Will Baptist denomination.

BIBLIOGRAPHY

Books

Adams, Jay E. *Pastoral Leadership.* Grand Rapids, Michigan: Baker Book House, 1975.

Allen, Roland. *Missionary Methods: St. Paul's or Ours?* Grand Rapids, Michigan: William B. Eerdmans, 1962.

Andelin, Aubrey P. *Man of Steel and Velvet.* Santa Barbara, California: Pacific Press, 1977.

Anderson, Andy. *Where Action Is.* Nashville, Tennessee: Broadman Press, 1976.

A Treatise of the Faith and Practices of the Original Free Will Baptists. Nashville, Tennessee: Executive Office, National Association of Free Will Baptists, 1977.

Barnes, Albert. *Barnes Notes on the New Testament.* Vol. 3, *Barnes Notes on Acts.* Grand Rapids, Michigan: Baker Book House, 1956.

Bedsole, Adolph. *The Pastor in Profile.* Grand Rapids, Michigan: Baker Book House, 1958.

Beebe, Wally. *All About the Bus Ministry.* Murfreesboro, Tennessee: Sword of the Lord Publishers, 1970.

_____. *All About the Second Man.* Murfreesboro, Tennessee: Sword of the Lord Publishers, 1971.

Benjamin, Paul. *The Growing Congregation.* Lincoln, Illinois: Lincoln Christian College Press, 1972.

Bisagno, John R. *How to Build an Evangelistic Church.* Nashville, Tennessee: Broadman Press, 1972.

_____. *The Power of Positive Evangelism.* Nashville, Tennessee: Broadman Press, 1968.

Brunner, Paul C. *Welcome to the Backyard..* Wilson, North

Carolina: Peace Free Will Baptist Church, 1977.

Clark, Wayne C. *The Minister Looks at Himself.* Chicago: The Judson Press, 1957.

Colsten, Elaine. *As I See Church Music.* Hammond, Indiana: Hyles-Anderson Publishers, 1969.

Crowe, J. M. and Merrill D. Moore. *Church Finance Record System Manual.* Nashville, Tennessee: Broadman Press, 1959.

Directory of Free Will Baptist Churches. Nashville, Tennessee: Free Will Baptist Executive Department, 1977.

Dodd, Damon C. *The Free Will Baptist Story.* Nashville, Tennessee: Free Will Baptist Executive Department, 1956.

Dollar, Truman. *How to Carry Out God's Stewardship Plan.* Nashville, Tennessee: Thomas Nelson Publishers, 1974.

Edwards, Gene. *How to Have a Soul Winning Church.* Montrose, California: Soul Winning Publications, 1962.

Engstrom, Ted W. and Edward R. Dayton. *The Art of Management for Christian Leaders.* Waco, Texas: Word Book Publishers, 1976.

Falwell, Jerry. *Capturing a Town for Christ.* Old Tappan, New Jersey: Fleming H. Revell, 1973.

_____ and Elmer Towns. *Church Aflame.* Nashville, Tennessee: Impact Books, 1971.

_____. *Youth Aflame.* Lynchburg, Virginia: Thomas Road Baptist Church, 1975.

Fisk, C. W. *Fruit That Remains.* Hammond, Indiana: First Baptist Church, 1975.

Friend, Fred E. *Standards for Day Care Centers.* Nashville, Tennessee: Department of Public Welfare, 1973.

Furlow, Elaine S. and Don Rutledge. *Love With No Strings.* Atlanta, Georgia: Home Mission Board, Southern Baptist

Convention, 1977.

_____. *The Human Touch.* Atlanta, Georgia: Home Mission Board, Southern Baptist Convention, 1977.

Gentry, Gardiner. *Bus Them In.* Nashville, Tennessee: Church Growth Publishers, 1973.

Gerber, Vergil. *A Manual for Evangelism/Church Growth.* South Pasadena, California: William Carey Library, 1973.

_____. *God's Way to Keep a Church Going and Growing.* South Pasadena, California: William Carey Library, 1973.

Godfrey, George. *Helps to Have a Soul Winning Church.* Crown Point, Indiana: Hyles-Anderson College, 1976.

_____. *How to Win Souls and Influence People for Heaven.* Hammond, Indiana: First Baptist Church, 1973.

Green, Hollis L. *Why Churches Die.* Minneapolis, Minnesota: Bethany Fellowship, 1972.

Gunther, Peter F. *The Fields at Home.* Chicago: Moody Press, 1963.

Harrison, Harrold D. *Commissioned to Communicate.* Nashville, Tennessee: Free Will Baptist Sunday School Department, 1969.

Hendrix, Olan. *Management and the Christian Worker.* Manila, Philippines: Church Literature Crusade International, 1972.

Hill, William. *Organizing and Developing a Free Will Baptist Sunday School.* Nashville, Tennessee: Free Will Baptist Sunday School Department, 1969.

Hodges, Melvin L. *Build My Church.* Springfield, Missouri: Foreign Missions Department of Assemblies of God, 1957.

_____. *On The Mission Field, The Indigenous Church.* Chicago: Moody Press, 1953.

Howse, W. L. *A Church Organized and Functioning.* Nashville,

Tennessee: Convention Press, 1963.

Hunter, Emily. *Christian Charm Course.* Portland, Oregon: Manna Publications, 1975.

Hunter, Wayne. *Man in Demand.* Portland, Oregon: Manna Publications, 1975.

Hutson, Curtis. *Pastors' and Workers' Conference.* Decatur, Georgia: Forrest Hills Baptist Church, n.d.

Hyles, Dave. *Successful Youth Work.* Murfreesboro, Tennessee: Sword of the Lord Publishers, 1976.

Hyles, Jack. *Church Bus Handbook.* Hammond, Indiana: Hyles-Anderson Publishers, 1970.

_____. *How To Boost Your Church Attendance.* Grand Rapids, Michigan: Zondervan Publishing House, 1958.

_____. *Let's Build An Evangelistic Church.* Murfreesboro, Tennessee: Sword of the Lord Publishers, 1962.

_____. *Let's Go Soul Winning.* Murfreesboro, Tennessee: Sword of the Lord Publishers, 1962.

_____. *Let's Use Letters and Forms.* Murfreesboro, Tennessee: Sword of the Lord Publishers, 1966.

_____. *The Hyles Church Manual.* Murfreesboro, Tennessee: Sword of the Lord Publishers, 1968.

_____. *The Hyles Sunday School Manual.* Murfreesboro, Tennessee: Sword of the Lord Publishers, 1969.

_____. *The Hyles Visitation Manual.* Hammond, Indiana: Hyles-Anderson Publishers, 1975.

Jaffray, George R., Jr. *Explosive Evangelism.* Mac Dill Air Force Base, Florida: Tyndale Bible Society, 1972.

Jernigan, Jules Donald. *Quest for the Rainbow.* Grand Rapids, Michigan: Baker Book House, 1975.

Johnson, Stanley C. *Church Extension Handbook.* Forest Park, Illinois: North American Baptist Missionary Society, 1973.

Jones, Bill. *Free Will Baptist Missions, Missionaries, and Their Message.* Nashville, Tennessee: Free Will Baptist Sunday School Department, 1972.

Kennedy, James D. *Evangelism Explosion.* Wheaton, Illinois: Tyndale House Publishers, 1970.

Kent, Homer A., Sr. *The Pastor and His Work.* Chicago: Moody Press, 1963.

Kilgore, Robert H. *How Much A Debtor.* Atlanta, Georgia: Home Mission Board, Southern Baptist Convention, 1973.

Knight, Walker, and Ken Touchton. *Seven Beginnings.* Atlanta, Georgia: Home Mission Board, Southern Baptist Convention, 1977.

Lebsack, Lee. *Ten at the Top.* Stow, Ohio: New Hope Press, 1974.

Loucks, Celeste, and Everett Hullum. *American Montage.* Atlanta, Georgia: Home Mission Board, Southern Baptist Convention, 1977.

Lovett, C. S. *Soul Winning Made Easy.* Baldwin Park, California: Personal Christianity, 1959.

MacNair, Donald J. *The Birth, Care, and Feeding of a Local Church.* Grand Rapids, Michigan: Baker Book House, 1971.

Malone, Tom. *Essentials of Evangelism.* Murfreesboro, Tennessee: Sword of the Lord Publishers, 1958.

_____. *The Sunday School Reaching Multitudes.* Murfreesboro, Tennessee: Sword of the Lord Publishers, 1973.

Martinez, Angel. *The Fountain of Youth.* Grand Rapids, Michigan: Zondervan Publishing House, 1957.

Massey, Craig W. *How to do Effective Visitation.* Wheaton, Illinois: Scripture Press, 1961.

McGavran, Donald A. *How Churches Grow.* New York: Friendship Press, 1955.

_____. and Win Arn. *How to Grow a Church.* Glendale, California: Regal Books, 1973.

McNeill, George S., editor. *The Sunday School Encyclopedia.* Vol. 12. Wheaton, Illinois: National Sunday School Association, 1965.

Molloy, John T. *Dress for Success.* New York: Warner Communications, 1975.

Moore, Mark. *The Ministry of Ushering.* Kansas City, Missouri: Beacon Hill Press, 1970.

Neithold, Eugene C. *Church Business Policies Outlined.* Greenville, South Carolina: Church Books, 1976.

Nevius, John L. *Planting and Development of Missionary Churches.* Nutley, New Jersey: The Presbyterian and Reformed Publishing Company, 1958.

Newman, Joseph. *How to Buy Real Estate.* Washington, D. C.: U. S. News and World Report, 1973.

Palmer, Bernard. *Pattern for a Total Church.* Wheaton, Illinois: Victor Books, 1973.

Parrott, Leslie. *Building Today's Church.* Grand Rapids, Michigan: Baker Book House, 1973.

Postal Service Manual. Washington, D. C.: U. S. Government Printing Office, 1977.

Powell, Ivor. *Don't Lose That Fish.* Grand Rapids, Michigan: Zondervan Publishing House, 1960.

Powell, William A. *The Urban Church Survey Manual.* Atlanta, Georgia: Home Mission Board, Southern Baptist Convention, 1972.

Publicity Handbook. Ft. Worth, Texas: Sperry and Hutchinson Company, 1972.

Rand McNally Road Atlas. Chicago: Rand McNally and

Company, 1976.

Reeds, Roger, editor. *Attack.* Nashville, Tennessee: Randall House Publications, 1977.

Rice, John R. *Why Our Churches Do Not Win Souls.* Murfreesboro, Tennessee: Sword of the Lord Publishers, 1966.

Risley, Clate A. and W. Donald Reeder, (eds.). *The Sunday School Encyclopedia.* Vol. 11. Chicago: National Sunday School Association, 1962.

Roberson, Lee. *The Witness Book.* Chattanooga, Tennessee: Highland Park Baptist Church, 1965.

Schuller, Robert H. *Your Church Has Real Possibilities.* Glendale, California: Regal Books, 1974.

Schwartz, David J. *The Magic of Thinking Big.* New York: Cornerstone Library, 1959.

Scott, Charles W. H., and others. *The Modern Pioneer.* Springfield Missouri: Assemblies of God Home Missions Department, 1967.

Smith, Wilbur. *The Minister in His Study.* Chicago: Moody Press, 1973.

Snyden, Howard F., and Warren W. Wiersbe. *When the Pastor Wonders How.* Chicago: Moody Press, 1973.

Spurgeon, Charles Haddon. *The Soul Winner.* Grand Rapids, Michigan: William B. Eerdmans Publishing Company, 1963.

Taylor, Kenneth. *Ministers' Research Service.* Wheaton, Illinois: Tyndale House Publishers, 1970.

The Executive's Complete Portfolio of Letters. Waterford, Connecticut: Bureau of Business Practice, 1976.

Thiessen, John Caldwell. *Pastoring the Smaller Church.* Grand Rapids, Michigan: Zondervan Publishing House, 1962.

Towns, Elmer. *America's Fastest Growing Churches.* Nashville,

Tennessee: Impact Books, 1972.

———. *Evangelize Thru Christian Education*. Wheaton, Illinois: Evangelical Teacher Training Association, 1970.

———. *Getting a Church Started in the Face of Insurmountable Odds with Limited Resources in Unlikely Circumstances*. Nashville, Tennessee: Impact Books, 1975.

———. *The Successful Sunday School and Teacher's Guidebook*. Carol Stream, Illinois: Creation House, 1976.

———. *The Ten Largest Sunday Schools*. Grand Rapids, Michigan: Baker Book House, 1969.

———. *Tithing is Christian*. Atlanta, Georgia: Sunday School Research Institute, 1975.

———. *World's Largest Sunday School*. Nashville, Tennessee: Thomas Nelson, Inc., 1974.

Underwood, Charles M., (ed.) *Planting the Independent Fundamental Church*. Greenville, South Carolina: Bob Jones University, 1972.

Vineyard, Jim, and Jerry Falwell. *Winning Souls Through Buses*. Nashville, Tennessee: Impact Books, 1972.

———. *World's Largest Junior Church*. Hammond, Indiana: First Baptist Church, 1974.

Wacker, Lyle, and others. *Church Extension Handbook*. Forest Park, Illinois: North American Baptist Missionary Society, n.d.

Wagner, C. Peter. *Your Church Can Grow*. Glendale, California: Gospel Light Publications, 1976.

Wardell, Don. *Practical Help for Christian Workers*. Winona Lake, Indiana: Wardell Publishers, 1974.

Westing, Harold J. *Make Your Sunday School Grow Through Evaluation*. Wheaton, Illinois: Victor Books, 1976.

Yamamori Tetsunao, and E. LeRoy Lawson. *Church Growth:*

Everybody's Business. Cincinnati, Ohio: Standard Publishing Company, 1973.

_____. *Introducing Church Growth.* Cincinnati, Ohio: Standard Publishing Company, 1975.

Pamphlets

Burden, Dale. *Workers Covenant.* Norfolk, Virginia: Fairmount Park Free Will Baptist Church, n.d.

Howard, Donald R., (ed.). *Facts About Accelerated Christian Education.* Garland, Texas: ACE, Incorporated, 1976.

Lilly, Tom. *Building a New Church.* Nashville, Tennessee: Free Will Baptist Home Missions Department, 1971.

Rice, Grant C. *Principles of New Church Planting.* Rockvale, Tennessee: Grant C. Rice Church Planting-Consulting, 1977.

Shockey, Robert L., (ed.).*The Sunday School Teachers Guide.* Nashville, Tennessee: Free Will Baptist Home Missions Department, 1975.

Thomas, Roy L. *Do You Know the Facts of Life?* Nashville, Tennessee: Free Will Baptist Home Missions Department, 1973.

_____. and Trymon Messer. *Follow Up Lessons for New Converts to Christ.* Nashville, Tennessee: Free Will Baptist Home Missions Department, 1972.

_____. *Free Will Baptist Home Missions Survey.* Nashville, Tennessee: Free Will Baptist Home Missions Department, 1974.

_____. *How to Get Visitors Cards.* Nashville, Tennessee: Free Will Baptist Home Missions Department, 1974.

268

———. *How to Give a Public Invitation.* Nashville, Tennessee: Free Will Baptist Home Missions Department, 1974.

———. *How to Have a Missions Conference in the Local Church.* Nashville, Tennessee: Free Will Baptist Home Missions Department, 1977.

———. *How to Prepare for Revival.* Nashville, Tennessee: Free Will Baptist Home Missions Department, 1977.

———. *How to Start a Church from Scratch.* Nashville, Tennessee: Free Will Baptist Home Missions Department, 1972.

———. *How to Use the Follow Up Lessons.* Nashville, Tennessee: Free Will Baptist Home Missions Department, 1972.

———. *How to Use the Tract, Do You Know the Facts of Life?* Nashville, Tennessee: Free Will Baptist Home Missions Department, 1973.

———. *Missions on the Move.* Nashville, Tennessee: Free Will Baptist Home Missions Department, 1978.

———. *The Home Mission Church and Finances.* Nashville, Tennessee: Free Will Baptist Home Missions Department, 1976.

———. *The Hunger in North America.* Nashville, Tennessee: Free Will Baptist Home Missions Department, 1974.

———. *Working at the Altar.* Nashville, Tennessee: Free Will Baptist Home Missions Department, 1969.

Willis, Homer E. *Why Home Missions.* Nashville, Tennessee: Free Will Baptist Home Missions Department, 1969.

Periodicals

Arn, Win, and David McGavran. "Planned Parenthood." *Church Growth: America.* September/October, 1976, p. 7.

Beebe, Wally, (ed.). *Church Bus News.* June/July 1976, pp. 8, 9.

Farnum, Granville W., (ed.). *The Sermon Builder.* March 1978, p. 2.

Guide to Proven Church Development Aids. 1977, pp. 8, 9.

Hughes, Blaine. "Are You Ready to Start a Christian School?" *Contact Magazine.* October 1975, p. 2.

Knight, Walker, (ed.). *Home Missions.* May 1976, pp. 25-32.

Lyon, Ruth A. (ed.). *Christ For All.* March/April 1977, p. 1.

_____. *Reach Out.* March/April 1977, pp. 2, 3.

McAllister, Jim. "Points for Pastors." *The Gem.* January 1977, p. 5.

Ohlin, John V. "A Church Is Born." *Church Growth: America.* September/October 1976, pp. 12, 13.

Shockey, Robert L., (ed.). *Mission Grams.* January/February 1978, p. 1.

The Minister's Practical Idea-Kit. 1978, p. 1.

Tapes

Helton, Max. "Acquiring a Building." Hammond, Indiana: Helton Publications, n.d.

_____. "Biblical Church Organization." Hammond, Indiana: Helton Publications, n.d.

_____. "Constitution and By-Laws." Hammond, Indiana: Helton Publications, n.d.

_____. "How to Get Set Up." Hammond, Indiana: Helton

Publications, n.d.

———. "How to Make an Offer on a Building." Hammond, Indiana: Helton Publications, n.d.

———. "Questions Most Often Asked." Hammond, Indiana: Helton Publications, n.d.

———. "Raising Support." Hammond, Indiana: Helton Publications, n.d.

———. "The Budget." Hammond, Indiana: Helton Publications, n.d.

———. "The First Sunday." Hammond, Indiana: Helton Publications, n.d.

———. "The Key to Getting Started Right." Hammond, Indiana: Helton Publications, n.d.

———. "The Kind of Sermons to Preach." Hammond, Indiana: Helton Publications, n.d.

———. "Where to Go." Hammond, Indiana: Helton Publications, n.d.

Printed in the United States
30973LVS00006B/116

9 780892 650705